Abolish Profits Taxes!

Abolish Profits Taxes!

By Loren Meierding

iUniverse, Inc.

New York   Bloomington

Abolish Profits Taxes!

iUniverse books may be ordered through booksellers or by contacting:

iUniverse
1663 Liberty Drive
Bloomington, IN 47403
www.iuniverse.com
1-800-Authors (1-800-288-4677)

ISBN: 978-1-4401-4884-2 (pbk)
ISBN: 978-1-4401-4883-5 (ebk)

Printed in the United States of America

iUniverse rev. date: 8/19/2009

Table of Contents

Forward

The current recession probably began around December of 2007. A large part of the problem was caused by the collapse of a bubble in the housing market that had been exacerbated by government regulatory action. As a consequence credit markets have shrunk and homebuyers and consumers have trouble borrowing money. The Obama answer to the problem is a Keynesian spending stimulus of trillions. While Obama and other Democrats made much of increases in the national debt by George Bush over a period of 8 years, Obama will outdo him in deficit spending by a factor of four.

Unfortunately, the Keynesian policy to turn around recessions by government spending has a grave deficiency. It may temporarily encourage some consumers to spend more, but in the longer run the government must borrow money that private entrepreneurs might have used to invest in new factories and equipment. By obstructing actions that would have employed many people permanently, the government slows down long term recovery and makes everyone poorer in the long run.

The most important action to turn around the recession and to improve long term growth as well, is to cut taxes, especially profits taxes. It is difficult to understand how someone who really was interested in being bipartisan as Obama claims he is, would not want to include tax cuts with spending to promote economic recovery. Why not include something that Republicans can support? Eliminating profits taxes would cause other countries to follow suit and would cause greater global economic growth. This book was written in the hope that it could help people see that there is much to gain by getting rid of profits taxes and very little to lose, except temporarily some tax revenue, which can be compensated for in a few years from increased economic growth. Although some have proposed cutting the Federal profits tax from 35 percent to 25 percent, why not do it right and go all the way for maximum short term and long term benefits? Doing so will surely promote global economic growth for great benefit to mankind. Failing to do so may prolong worldwide economic difficulties and even encourage some wars.

Chapter 1—Overview

The purpose of this book is to convince people that abolishing profits taxes should be done now. It should be done now, if only for the long term benefit of the U.S. Since it would also force other countries to follow suit, it would be of great benefit for the whole world as well. Companies would have more money for investment and less need for borrowing. There would be stronger saving and investment and better long term growth. If this is not done the U.S. and world economies will be exposed to greater risks.

There are very great short term benefits. Stock market price-earnings ratios would automatically drop and cause an immediate stock market rise. Companies would have more money immediately available for investment. Companies with funding constraints would have more of their own money available for investment. During the current credit collapse, companies would have more of their own money available. With the economy in recession abolishing profits taxes would stimulate the economy to come out of recession like nothing else. Of course an even better move would be to transform the tax code by moving entirely from income taxes to consumption taxes eliminating all taxation of saving and investment. It is saving and investment that produces growth in the economy and growth in productivity, wages, and salaries so that people have more after tax income and better living standards in the long run. But replacing income taxes is a political task that will probably take decades. It would be very easy to abolish profits taxes. Since businesses are responsible for the bulk of saving and investment anyway, eliminating profits taxes would be a great boon to our economy. Other countries would need to follow suit greatly strengthening world wide economic growth. There are many reasons for abolishing profits taxes which are covered in Chapters 10 through 13. Some readers might want to go directly to those chapters.

Section 1 shows why it is important to maintain free markets with minimal government intervention. It presumes that economic growth and raising our standards of living should be a primary goal so that virtually everyone benefits. Chapter 2 covers factors that govern a free economy and the important role that profits play. Chapter 3 points out reasons why government intervention and regulation is damaging to an economy. We have an economy with considerable detrimental government meddling. While the left blames capitalism and corporations for problems, the truth of the matter is that the problems mostly result from the activity of government, as was the case in the 2008-2009 recession (see Chapter 9). Chapter 4 discusses key incentives in our economy and some of the impacts when government modifies them.

Section 2 considers objections to economic growth as a primary goal and argues that the objections are unjustified. Obviously an underlying assumption in this book is that strong economic growth, growth in productivity, and growth in living standards is desirable. Economic growth will achieve the most good to improve the lives of those in our society who are poorer and have weak skills. Global economic growth is important for the well being of the poor in third world countries. Many on the left contest the desirability of more growth. They want to cut back because they think that we are destroying the planet by burning fossil fuels and that our resources are running out. They advocate wasting vast amounts of resources to try to reduce emissions without moral justification. Such beliefs have little basis in fact. There is little warrant for taking any actions to reduce our standard of living. We should seek economic growth not only for ourselves, but for the whole world. Free markets will solve future problems by providing enough resources. There is every reason to believe that resources are essentially infinite. Chapter 5 indicates why we should seek strong economic growth. Although we cannot prove that we may not run out of some resource in the future, we should not worry about running out of resources. Chapter 6 discusses why we should not stymie growth from worries about climate change.

Section 3 takes up the question of government policy responses to recessions that rely on stimulus packages. Chapter 7 discusses the business cycle arguing that although business cycles are virtually unavoidable, the booms and busts are self-correcting. Chapter 8 considers the question of whether government creates jobs and argues that it has very little to do with job creation other than to redirect spending into unproductive uses that are less valuable to society. A major claim by those who want the government to spend to end recessions and to meddle in the economy in general is that government will create jobs, millions of them in fact. Chapter 9 considers Obama's Keynesian stimulus plan and shows why it is unlikely to do much for the economy. If Obama really wanted to get us out of our current malaise he would abolish the profits tax.

Section 4 gives reasons why profits taxes are so undesirable. They are bad for economic growth and raising standards of living and should be abolished. Thus, Chapters 10 to 13 show why profits taxes are bad for the economy and why abolishing the profits tax is desirable to combat recession and to enhance long term growth.

For all of my lifetime Democrats have pointed their fingers at Republicans and claimed that the Republican Party is the party of Big Business and that Republicans care about the corporations and not about the "average Joe." This claim has been made so many times that, like all propaganda constantly repeated, most people tend to believe it. This belief is probably so ingrained that it will take decades to be reversed. But Chapter 14 shows that, in fact, the policies of the Democratic Party cause reduced competition in the marketplace and concentration of power in Big Business. The Republicans are not guiltless, but the Democratic Party is committed not only to concentrating power in the Federal Government, but also in concentrating power in Big Business and the multinational corporations. Chapter 15 simply sums up the conclusions.

Section 1—
Free Markets and Government Intervention

Chapter 2—The Importance of Economic Freedom

What Makes an Economy Productive?

If we wish to promote better standards of living for our citizens, we need to ask what conditions will best promote the necessary economic growth required to achieve it. There are at least eight conditions needed: 1) opportunities to provide services people want, 2) private parties possessing strong property rights that can take advantage of those opportunities, 3) available capital that can be invested to produce the goods or services desired, 4) good reason to believe that investing the capital will provide a return or profit over and above the invested capital, 5) corporations that have the capacity to engage in large enterprises with limited liability for shareholders, 6) many industrious people and corporations willing to compete with one another to improve market share and profits, 7) a medium of exchange to facilitate buying, selling, and borrowing, and 8) a government that protects life and property and provides national defense.

All the conditions are important. Since people have many interests and desires, there are many ways to provide a service they will pay for if they can. Private persons who can expect personal gain from entrepreneurial activity will produce much more than persons who do not personally benefit from engaging in economic activities. Corporations are necessary because many products that can be produced require the effort of many people and on a scale that no stockholder can have personal liability. Private property is needed so individuals and corporations can borrow to invest and can keep profits they obtain. Otherwise, there is no incentive to engage in productive activities beyond providing bare necessities for living. A medium of exchange greatly facilitates enterprise and obtaining capital to invest. We take these conditions for granted in modern developed economies.

Private businesses both small and large are the engines that provide jobs and economic growth. We should attend especially to their needs to ensure conditions are optimal for their growth. Then the jobs they provide will be good jobs and provide the best growth in productivity, so that people's living standards grow the most. That is also the best way to help the poorer members of a society.

Capital Investment

We need to consider more carefully four of the conditions above. A first major condition is: *available capital can be invested to produce the goods or services desired*. Indeed, the more capital that has been accumulated the more tools and opportunities are available to be productive. Countries that have more capital can produce more and will have more to share and have a higher standard of living.

A second condition is *the activities that persons invest in must give them reasons to believe that they will obtain a profit* so they will have something to show for committing their capital to producing goods and services. Effort is wasted if it does not provide income that can be spent for things needed and desired. Capital is employed to produce some return, something additional of value. If there were no expectation that the capital would produce some additional return, it would not be employed. The return on the capital is the profit. We need to have economic policies that promote investment to induce strong productivity growth. Since investment is correlated with profits, we should also promote strong profits. A beauty of free market capitalism is that strong competition in the marketplace prevents profits from being excessive for very long.

The Benefits from Strong Market Competition

A third condition is *the stronger the competition between individuals and corporations to provide better products and services, the better those products will be.* The opportunity to obtain a better profit spurs innovation and efficient use of resources. Strong competition among many motivated entrepreneurs with opportunities to provide better products puts many of the least skilled to work. If regulations do not stand in the way, entrepreneurs will train the people they need to make products.

One important fact that is not understood by those on the left is that freed markets promote efficient use of resources and minimal wastage of resources while government bureaucrats waste them like crazy. Whenever entrepreneurs provide a product or service, those products and services require using resources that were acquired at some cost. Free market systems encourage entrepreneurs to minimize their costs to maximize their profits. If the entrepreneur is to minimize his costs and maximize his profits, he has an incentive to use the resources he needs in the most efficient manner possible. A couple of examples illustrate this phenomenon.

John D. Rockefeller succeeded in obtaining 90% of the oil refining market for a period of time. He did so because he found ways to convert virtually the entire barrel of crude oil into various products. He did not need to dispose of residues causing pollution of the environment. But his competitors had residues that did pollute the environment. Since he produced more products out of a barrel of oil than his competitors, he could sell kerosene and later gasoline for a lower price than his competitors. Laissez-faire free market competition induced him to use minimal resources and to not pollute the environment.

A second example of market competition encouraging the most efficient use of resources is the development of the aluminum can for beer and soda pop. When aluminum cans first came on the marketplace the cans were much heavier than they are now. The market encouraged the companies that produced the cans and the bottling companies to come up with ways to use less aluminum in the cans. Since firms like Coca Cola sell billions of cans of soft drinks in a year, removing just a sliver of aluminum from every can, can mean hundreds of thousands of dollars in savings and in additional profit. So over time the aluminum can has gotten lighter and lighter. Much less aluminum is used now for a comparable number of cans than forty years ago. Without the incentive of profits the innovations would not have occurred.

Innovation

Free market competition does allow very enterprising companies starting or developing new innovations to take very large shares of an industry for a period of time. As noted John D. Rockefeller was able to get 90% of the crude oil refining market during the Nineteenth Century. He did so by finding ways to process virtually all of a barrel of crude oil into various products. He could charge the lowest prices and still make good profits. Many competitors were not nearly as efficient and could not compete with his prices.

The wonderful thing about markets that are free is that entrepreneurs have incentives to innovate and invent new products that may appeal to people. If the new products or services appeal to people, the entrepreneur who has invested in providing them will at first have little competition and will be able to earn high profits. But very soon other entrepreneurs will see that the new market provides high profits and will compete. Soon when supply has caught up to the demand, the prices will drop and those providing the good or service will only be able to earn average profits. Usually this happens fairly quickly. But in some cases like that of Standard Oil, the entrepreneur is able to dominate for some time before losing its dominant position. Standard Oil's market share of refining fell from 90% in 1880 to 60% in 1911 when antitrust action split it into many companies. IBM had a dominance in the computer field for a long time.

Using free markets will solve problems of obtaining energy resources more quickly. Government management of the process will slow it down. The best approach is to remove corporate profits taxes so that energy companies have more to invest to find the new sources. Restrictions on use of nuclear power and drilling for oil need to be removed. In due time sources of energy will be found and our dependence on foreign sources will be reduced. If we use government rather than the private sector in an attempt to hasten the process, we will waste large amounts of investment funds on boondoggles and will slow down the process.

Role of Government

A fourth key condition is: *government needs to protect the persons and property of citizens and provide a legal system, but it should stay out of the economy as much as possible.* With the greatest amount of economic freedom, there will be the greatest economic growth. Government usually intervenes in ways that reduce investment, cause misallocation of resources, interfere with the freedom of economic actors, and place unnecessary burdens on the economy. A laissez-faire environment provides more freedom for everyone. It is more efficient. An immense amount of our resources today are wasted by bureaucrats. Private investment frees up more resources for saving and investment and there is better growth in productivity and incomes.

Ensuring strong competition by avoiding government meddling in the economy keeps profits at an adequate level but prevents excessive profits. Strong competition provides environments where every person's work is solicited and needed. There undoubtedly will always be some abuses by corporate leaders, but introducing regulations and regulatory agencies reduces competition and long term growth to everyone's detriment. Regulation provides more opportunities for and encourages more corruption. Strong competition in the marketplace does a better job of policing businesses than government regulators ever will.

Government Allocation of Resources

It has been proven many times that entrepreneurs in the private sector are best at solving various problems. When there is a problem that people want solved badly enough to pay for the solution, a free market system will give incentives to entrepreneurs to come up with a solution and to invest money. They invest on the expectation that they will earn a good return for providing the needed solution. Government bureaucrats do not have incentives to really provide solutions. However sincere they may be, they do not spend the public's money with the same care that they would spend their own. Certainly they do not spend as carefully as private entrepreneurs would spend their profits.

When government bureaucrats spend investment money from the taxpayers they do not have incentives to be efficient. Even if they are environmentalists committed to being "green," they will be much more wasteful of resources. Wasting resources makes everyone poorer in the long run.

When government directs investment decisions mistakes are invariably made. Consider the decision by the Bush Administration to promote ethanol production from corn for additives to gasoline to reduce dependence on foreign energy sources. Government was directing spending and investment in the economy. It diverted investment in one resource to another resource. Of course the demand for corn had to go up and the price of corn rose. Since corn is a staple and is used to feed livestock, its price affects the price of many food products. It affects food prices not only in the U.S., but especially in the Third World. As a result of the U.S. subsidies for ethanol and laws requiring that it be mixed with gasoline many people in the world are having trouble finding the means to feed themselves adequately.

There are many resources that show inelasticity of supply, that is, there is a capacity limitation on producing them, and increasing their production takes considerable time. Consequently, if demand exceeds supply, or commodities traders believe it will, the price will spike upward as happened in 2008 for crude oil. Congress had banned offshore drilling and was resisting giving permission again. If government officials have incorrect ideas about various resources, they can cause prices to soar and reduce availability of needed resources. Officials are then responsible for reducing long term growth.

Value

The goods or services produced by the use of capital have a value to people that determines the price paid. Classical economists including Adam Smith believed product values were determined by the costs of production including labor, rents, and cost of capital used. Neoclassical economists for the last century and a quarter have a different concept of the source of value. It is a psychological concept. The value is determined as the utility things have for buyers—what it is worth to them or its usefulness to them. The value or utility products and services have for people determines their demand. The reason people may want to buy things does not necessarily depend on the cost to produce them. They may just want to keep up with the Jones. They may want to be a part of the latest fad and may pay a premium price for many items. Of course the demand depends also on what people have, usually in the form of money representing capital, that they can use to buy goods and services.

A fundamental assumption that economists make is that the price of any good or service reflects its utility and that goods or services with the same price are of equal value to society. Prices also determine where money is best invested. The price value, the volume of sales for particular products, the costs of production, and resulting potential profits determines where investments in the private sector are made.

Economists tend to assume that the prices government pays and the investments government makes are on par with prices and investments in the private sector. Although the assumption is natural and virtually unavoidable, it is questionable. Government responds to various political pressures and often pays more than goods and services are really worth.

Government contracts frequently go to insiders for prices that are too high. Investment decisions by private investors tend to find projects that best promote long term growth and have the greatest potential, because it is their own money they are putting at risk. But politicians and bureaucrats will spend money on projects because some special interest desires it. The spending and investment is generally on items of poorer quality in the sense that they have less value to society. The fact that governments spend on things that people have not been willing to pay for with their own money is an indication that government often spends on things that are not of long term value and not helpful for economic growth. When decisions go through a political process, one should expect less beneficial projects to emerge.

The Importance of Profits

It is important to adequately appreciate the role of profits. Keynesian economics emphasizes the propensity to consume function defining the amount of income consumers spend. Investment is largely determined by the level of consumption because it is needed to replace depreciating equipment that produces consumer products and services. The overall level of investment, according to Keynes depends on the marginal efficiency of capital and its expected yield being above the interest rate.[1] Since profits equal sales minus the costs, the long term profits from an investment determines the viability of the investment. But because we cannot determine future earnings of capital exactly, it is the entrepreneur's *expectation* of the earnings of capital that determines whether he will invest. While Keynes seems to take the importance of profits fairly seriously, many of his followers seem to overlook their importance. For example, if one examines Paul Samuelson's Economics, the primary U.S. introductory economics textbook for decades, the first discussion of profits is a short 4 pages first discussed 660 pages into an 895 page book.[2] But profits drive free market economies. Adam Smith devotes a long chapter early in The Wealth of Nations to profits.

It is exceedingly important to avoid interfering with profits if they are to have their proper incentive effects. Neoclassical economics assumes that companies try to maximize their profits.[3] This may include any capital gains. Although it seems reasonable to believe that companies try to maximize their profits, some business leaders might have more conservative approaches. Investors and companies have a choice between investing in relatively safe bonds earning interest versus investing in production where the return is a little riskier. Recent returns will factor into decisions to invest. In order to justify putting capital to use for production rather than at interest, the expected return on capital should exceed interest rates. This agrees with Keynes who held that the marginal efficiency of capital or the lifetime expected return on invested capital must equal interest rates.[4]

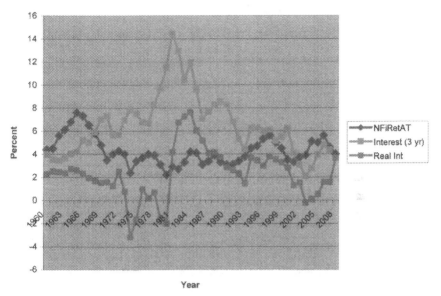

Figure 2-1—Returns to Capital

Figure 2-1 shows after tax returns on produced assets to U.S. domestic non-financial corporations with the middle line.[5] The interest rates for 3 Year U.S. Treasury Bonds are plotted with the upper line. The CPI-U index has been subtracted from the Treasury Bond rate to yield an estimate of real interest rates as shown by the lower line.[6] We may note that returns to non-financial corporations exceed the real interest rates except during the 1980's when real interest rates temporarily spiked upward. Since the value of assets produced increases with inflation, the best comparison to returns is with real interest rates. The returns to capital for the U.S. tend to be about 2 or 3 percent above real interest rates.

The returns undoubtedly would have been better with no profits taxes. During the 1980's and in recent years much investment has gone into real estate and financial assets instead of fixed investments. This should be expected if the returns to capital do not exceed real interest rates by very much.

Profits are very important for investment which is the primary factor determining economic growth. Figure 2-2 shows after tax profits for U.S. non-financial corporations and their level of investment as a percentage of the national income.[7] It is evident that there is a significant correlation of investment with after tax profits. As one might expect sometimes there is a lag of a year or so from a good year in profits to an increase in investment. We see a long term declining trend in terms of after tax profits of non-financial corporations as a share of national income. After the 1970's, manufacturing corporations shrank as a proportion of the economy. Service corporations, which tend to run lower profit margins, expanded their share. A slight increasing trend in investment is apparent if one takes the low period of the 1930's and 1940's into account. Since most investment is needed to replace depreciating assets, the relatively flat trend is to be expected. If corporations were able to keep all their profits we should expect to see more investment and more growth.

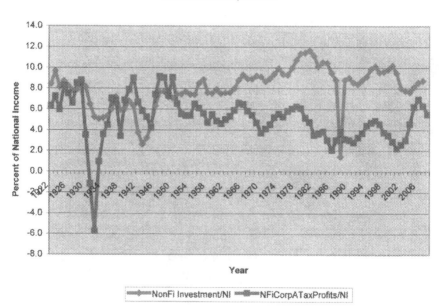

Figure 2-2 After Tax Profits and Investment
for U.S. Non-Financial Corporations

Figure 2-3 shows after-tax profits and investment for U.S. manufacturing corporations. In the case of U.S. manufacturing corporations one can again detect a correlation between increases and decreases in profits and investment.[8] The long term profits trend has been down for many years, but that just reflects the fact that since the 1970's the share of manufacturing corporations in the economy has fallen from about 22 percent to about 11 percent. Although one of the reasons for manufacturing corporations moving their operations overseas was to find cheaper labor, the presence of high U.S. profits taxes and lower taxes overseas surely was a significant factor. As will be argued in Chapter 4, the burden of profits taxation falls more heavily on manufacturing corporations than on service corporations. Because much heavier investments are required, the profits tax tends to shift investment from manufacturing to service industries.

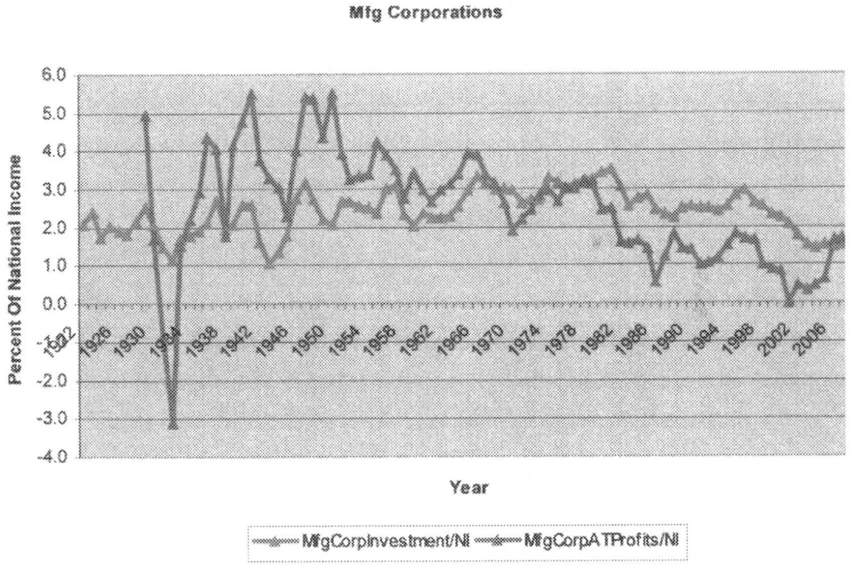

Mfg Corporations

Figure 2-3 Manufacturing Corporation After Tax Profits and Investment

Complaints About Laissez-Faire

As the industrial revolution developed in the Nineteenth Century in Britain and the United States, laissez-faire capitalism generally prevailed. It produced some conditions that sustained political movements and led to government interference in the market place. There were squalid living conditions for many workers. Young children were forced to work long hours in factories. Some entrepreneurs became exceedingly wealthy. Socialism became politically popular and caused some countries to nationalize industries and to institute considerable transfer payments to try to even out the wealth. In the Twentieth Century socialism was instituted on a grand sale in the Soviet Union and on a smaller scale by taxation and redistribution of wealth in capitalist countries like Sweden, Norway, Denmark, Germany, and France.

There are two major complaints about laissez-faire capitalism that we will take up in more detail in Chapter 3. First, it presumably produces considerable inequality and secondly greedy entrepreneurs presumably are able to exploit consumers and make large profits. Greedy corporate executives are paid excessively high salaries. Some on the left want to eliminate inequality and greed by implementing socialist economies. Most on the left want to introduce government regulations, regulators, and high taxation to redistribute income as has been done in social democracies like the Scandinavian countries and France. These countries operate on a capitalist basis, but have heavy levels of taxation and involvement of the government in the economy.

Critics of the United States economy argue that the U.S. has too much inequality and greed. They argue that since the Reagan revolution in the 1980's, inequality as measured by the Gini coefficient has increased. [9] The richest Americans have prospered much more than the middle class and poor. They want to increase tax rates on the rich to redistribute income and reduce inequality.

As will be argued in Chapter 3, high tax rates on the upper income will not necessarily do much to reduce economic inequality. Nor does regulation help reduce greed. Regulation usually provides more opportunities for corruption and often for using niches created by the law to earn more money and actually increase inequality.

Criticism of capitalism that takes the U.S. economy to be an example of laissez-faire capitalism is misplaced. As Milton Friedman liked to point out, the various government entities in the U.S. spend about 40% of the U.S. national income. If one figures that government regulations dictate spending for at least another 10%, one-half the U.S. economy is controlled by government. One might say that the U.S. economy is half "socialist." Although the Scandinavian countries and France have a higher ratio of government tax income to gross domestic product than the U.S.—the U.S. ratio of almost .4 to their nearly .5—the U.S. is not as far behind in size of government as many critics suppose.[10] Under the Obama Administration the U.S. is heading toward the democratic socialist level of government.

There is going to be considerable inequality in a laissez-faire capitalist economy. People's goals differ. Some are more committed to earning money and acquiring assets and things. Others just want to make enough to enjoy life. Some people are more committed to getting college degrees which tends to pay off in earning much higher incomes than those who get less education. Rewards in income should reflect effort, work, skill, and knowledge. It should have a connection to what one produces.

As we will see in Chapter 3 adding more taxation and regulation to the U.S. economy which already has a large burden of taxation and regulation, will not necessarily improve distribution. It is more likely that it will *reduce economic growth and make many people poorer in the long run than otherwise.*

Chapter 3—Problems with Socialism and Government Regulation

The advocate of a free market economy believes economic fairness means giving everyone equal opportunity to find and exploit their niche in the marketplace working with the level of effort they desire. They should expect to be rewarded in proportion to their effort, the contribution they make, and their utilization of acquired skills and knowledge.

The socialist on the other hand believes that fairness requires that everyone have relatively equal amounts of material possessions. Free market capitalism is what tends to happen if government does not intervene. Economic rewards will tend to be based on family effort, skills possessed, and earnings. Socialism, on the other hand, requires government force to redistribute products and services in the economy in a more equal fashion.

A brief discussion of true socialism that involves government control of an economy without free markets is in order, but the bulk of discussion must go to attempts to reduce or eliminate greed and inequality by heavy handed government taxation and regulation.

Socialism

By the end of the 1980's and the fall of the Soviet Union, it was evident that true socialism was a failure. Only capitalism really works. Only capitalism adequately ensures property rights to citizens. Socialism generally is popular for those who deny the existence of an afterlife. If there is no afterlife, then material possessions in this life are highly important. It then seems desirable that everyone should share about equally. Socialists incorrectly assume also that people are altruistic and can be motivated to work equally hard to produce goods that everyone will share.

But there are two problems. People are not fundamentally altruistic. Socialism changes the incentive to work. It does not reward people in proportion to their effort and contribution. There is no reward for innovation and improvement in efficiency. Consequently, under socialism better workers, who do not receive more for producing more, reduce their efforts. Less is produced and available for distribution and virtually everyone becomes poorer than under capitalism, which permits considerable inequality of incomes and possessions. If freedom or liberty is a preeminent goal of society and different people have different goals in life, we should expect differences in the amount and kind of possessions they acquire. The good things in life do not depend on acquiring lots of material possessions.

The second problem is that socialism has a different method of distribution than capitalism which distributes by the marketplace. What a person earns by selling his labor he can use to buy products. Socialism requires an elite to make distribution using government force. Under socialism there has to be a bureaucratic elite that decides how to invest capital resources and how to distribute what is produced. Neither job is done properly or well by people outside of a free market. In a purely socialistic system the elite do not have markets to tell them where investment needs to be made. Consequently lacking needed information, they waste resources on a grand scale. They also use their political position to gain special favors and privileges for themselves unavailable to the average person. While theoretically everyone had equal possessions belonging to the state, the Soviet Communist Party members had a much higher standard of living than the average Russian citizen.

Naïve socialists seem to think that there are lots of free lunches—that government can by progressive taxation, transfer payments, or other means, redistribute the goods and services in society without diminishing the pie to be divided up. They tend to think that employees and entrepreneurs will out of the goodness of their hearts produce every bit as much, even though many will receive much smaller shares of the pie. In fact there is a major change in the incentives to work when the monetary rewards for working hard are reduced. There will be a reduction in production even when relatively minor reductions in rewards for labor occur. The net result of implementing socialism is that much less is produced, the pie shrinks and nearly everyone is considerably poorer.

Socialists apparently believe that despite the fact that incentives to work are altered significantly and nearly everyone will be poorer, it just is fairer and better that everyone should have comparable shares of what is produced. Proposing implementation of an economic system that basically makes everyone poorer just so there will be a more equal distribution of goods, because it is supposedly fairer, seems morally ludicrous.

Today many on the left believe there is climate change from burning fossil fuels that require us to cut back on energy use. They believe we are running out of resources as another reason we should cut back on what we produce. But when one looks at the evidence in Chapters 5 and 6 about climate change and our resources, it is evident a rational person should conclude that we have no good reason to cut back on economic growth. It is foolishness to think that everyone needs to become poorer in order to save the planet.

Democratic Socialism

Since the fall of Communism in 1989, it has been apparent that true socialism has been a failure. Many still believe in a socialistic society that has a basically capitalist organization of the economy, but that a considerable part of income should be redistributed to bring more equality. They believe that government should provide health care and some services for everyone. Many believe that there is considerable market failure that government needs to step in and fix. Most European countries follow this model. They have high personal taxes especially in the Scandinavian countries. High personal tax rates tend to produce sluggish economies with slow growth and relatively high unemployment especially for young people.

It should be evident that high taxation reduces incentives to produce and to innovate. In the long run everyone in the society will have a lower standard of living than they might otherwise have had. Hence trying to impose a socialistic welfare state with a more equal distribution of goods and services because it is fairer seems quite dubious. Trying to impose it changes work incentives considerably. Since in the long run almost everyone is far better off with a laissez-faire approach and equal opportunity, that seems better and fairer in actuality.

Scandinavian countries still have capitalist ownership of the means of production and have generally a lower taxation of capital than the United States. They have very heavy taxation of personal income to provide government services. With the Progressive movement in the early Twentieth Century and FDR's New Deal, the role of government in the U.S. economy has greatly expanded. Now, in 2009, governments in the U.S. collect almost 40% of GDP to spend and redistribute. So we are far from being laissez-faire. Of course, even under laissez-faire, government needs to provide national defense and a judicial system. But government spending really need not be more than 10% of GDP. We could do quite well with less than 5% of the regulations that we have as well. Health care would be affordable for nearly everyone in a much larger economy.

Inequality of Money Income and Disposable Income

Reducing the connection between production and income by redistributionary taxation reduces incentives to produce. *It does not necessarily produce more equality.* Gini coefficients are often used to measure income or wealth inequality. A Gini coefficient of 0 represents a case with all persons having equal amounts of the quantity being measured and therefore perfect equality. A coefficient of 1 represents perfect inequality with one person having all the measured quantity and everyone else in the group having none of it. Thus the greater the value of the coefficient, the greater the inequality among members of the population. Since different countries have different regulations, methods of taxation, and methods of collecting data, calculated Gini coefficients are not precisely comparable. One must be careful to compare countries on money income or better on disposable income. The U.S. Census Bureau changed the method of collecting income data in 1993 which caused an increase of at least .02 in the Gini coefficient merely from change in method. This gives critics of capitalism the idea that an increase in income inequality has occurred over the past 20 years when in fact there really has not been a change.

Sweden, which has very heavy personal income taxes has a Gini coefficient for income distribution of .23.[1] Advocates of socialism or those desiring redistribution tend to quote the U.S. Gini coefficient of household income before taxes and income transfers as .45 which makes the inequality seem greater vis-à-vis other countries than its value after transfers of .38.[2] For 2005 a U.S. Gini coefficient of .418 was calculated.[3] Although it is true that the U.S. Gini coefficient is higher and implies more inequality of income than other developed countries and has increased some over the last 40 years, there are some considerations to be brought to bear on the matter to yield a proper perspective.

Gini coefficients applied to income distribution in countries for a one year period have significant defects. Ideally inequality measures should be based on lifetime incomes. For example, suppose all people in the U.S. had a pattern of income from age 20 to 64 like the author's. They would have many years in school and taking care of their parents with very small income and a number of years with quite high income. If all ages are represented, the Gini coefficient for the U.S. would be around .65 which shows significant inequality. In a given year many would have very low incomes and others fairly high incomes. Yet if everyone had this same pattern with the same incomes in constant dollars over their lifetimes, there would be perfect equality and the Gini coefficient would be zero if comparing lifetime incomes.

The U.S. had a comparably high Gini coefficient for incomes during the first decades of the Twentieth Century probably reaching a maximum in 1928 when the Gini coefficient for income must have exceeded .50. But with the crash of the stock market in 1929 and the Great Depression and World War II the upper income earners lost a large part of their income and the Gini coefficient for income fell significantly to .371 in 1948.[4] After World War II from 1947 to 1981, the U.S. Gini coefficient for aggregate income for families was relatively stable within a range from .348 (in 1968) to .379. From 1981 to 1992 it gradually increased from .369 to .404.[5]

The increase in the Gini coefficient in recent years for the U.S. does not necessarily indicate real changes in inequality. One post World War II trend is that many women entered the workforce. This has meant that many households have two or more earners whereas before the war most households were single earner households. Also many women take part time jobs to add extra income but may not want to work full time. After about 1960 divorce lost its stigma and there have been many more broken homes and single mothers. Single mothers frequently do not have an established occupation and usually earn substantially less than most other workers. Thus there is more variability of household earnings. These social and demographic trends will increase the Gini coefficient without necessarily being the result of unfairness or a defect of capitalism.

Household or family income tends to be used for estimating inequality. But given the variability in household units, the best unit for purposes of comparison is the individual. If full time year around workers in 1968 rather than households are considered, the Gini coefficient was .34, but in 2007 was .39.[6]

As a country becomes wealthier, real incomes increase, and household wealth increases. Some people may take a few years off during their working years with greatly reduced income to travel or to do volunteer work. More people are spending more time in schools than in the past. Trends like these will increase the Gini coefficient without really meaning that there is more inequality as far as lifetime earnings are concerned. These factors no doubt explain some of the increase in the Gini coefficient in the U.S. since World War II. Some of the increase may be from people spending more time getting educated and some working harder than others. Some of the increase then may be due to natural factors and differences in effort and goals.

A comparison of the differences in inequality of income between less socialistic countries like the U.S. and democratic socialist countries like Sweden must take into account the effects of redistributionary taxation through high taxes on upper income earners. An important factor in lowering the Gini coefficient is that when faced with high tax rates many who might otherwise produce more will cut work and enjoy less income bringing them down closer to the average in income. The economy of democratic socialistic countries will produce less than it would with less onerous taxation. People in the society will have lowered standards of living. The Gini coefficient will be lower and incomes will be more equal. But the people will be poorer.

Those who complain about relatively high or increasing Gini coefficients in capitalist economies often tend to assume that the same people remain in the lowest quintiles so that there is a permanent underclass. It is true that some people remain in the same quintile year after year. However, it is also true that there is a very great amount of mobility between quintiles. Some people have low incomes for a year or more and then get a much better paying job and move into higher quintiles. This phenomenon also occurs in many of the European countries. It is quite possible that from the standpoint of lifetime income the inequality is less than the Gini coefficients imply.

Some of the U.S. post-World War II increases in the Gini index can be attributed to increases in the generosity of welfare plans. When workers can live adequately without working due to generous welfare, even though they could earn more working some job, they may take the welfare. Since they earn less than they would if welfare had not been made more generous, inequality of income is increased and the Gini coefficient increases due to changes in work incentives instituted by Congress.

Inequality of Wealth

If the Gini coefficient is to be used to evaluate inequality, it is best used to evaluate distribution of wealth. Wealth tends to persist over time. Wealth tends to be rather unequally distributed. Many on the left look at the higher Gini coefficient than European countries and feel that to be more fair U.S. capitalism should have more government redistribution of income like Sweden, France, and Germany. The wealth held by the top 1 percent of U.S. citizens is 33% of all U.S. wealth. It is also true that Americans in the top 1 percent of all world wealthholders hold 37.4% of that wealth. Of 793 billionaires in the world 45% are Americans.[7] The case is similar for those with hundreds of millions. The wealthiest Americans earned the money due to the massive size of the American economy for the last six decades and the great opportunities. The greatest American companies became multinational companies that dominate many markets. The fact the wealth produced by what have been the world's greatest companies is centered in the United States is going to cause the U.S. Gini coefficients to show more inequality.

To view the matter in the best perspective it is useful to consider U.S. wealth Gini coefficients throughout our history. In rural areas of the U.S. the wealth Gini has been in the .6 to .7 range. Typically when land is newly settled the Gini coefficient tends to be around .6 and then increases. For example, in 1860, thirteen years after Utah was settled its wealth Gini was .62 and income Gini was .32. Ten years later the wealth Gini was .73 and in 1886 the income Gini was .44. In 1774 the wealth Gini for free wealthholders in the U.S. was .66. The Gini coefficient for wealth in the 1860 to 1870 period has been estimated at .83.[8]

The wealth Gini for the U.S. as a whole was probably around .83 for much of the Nineteenth Century and remained so until 1929. We should remember that during the Nineteenth Century the United States had less inequality than European countries. In regard to wealth the Nineteenth Century trend appears to have been toward greater inequality. But the disruptions of the Great Depression and World War II reduced the inequality. An estimate for 1962 for all households is .76.[9] The Gini coefficient for distribution of wealth in the U.S. in 2000 was .801.[10] The top 1 percent of wealthholders own about 33 percent of wealth and the top 5 percent about 71 percent.

The U.S. does now show a greater inequality than European countries with the exception of Switzerland which like the U.S. is less prone to engage in redistribution of wealth. Nevertheless, despite the level of redistribution in European countries, their wealth Gini coefficients are only moderately better than the U.S. The Gini wealth coefficient for France is .73 and .67 for Germany.[11] Even in a democratic socialist country like Sweden with very high personal tax rates and the greatest redistribution of income, the wealth Gini coefficient in 1978 was .78. It increased to .84 in the 1990's and reached .86 in 1999. In 2003 it was .85.[12] Twenty-four percent of the Swedish population have no net worth at all. In Sweden, the top 5 percent have 77 percent of the wealth and the top 1 percent have 38 percent. Perhaps without the devastation of World War II, France and Germany would have wealth distributions like Sweden's that are higher than the U.S.

It may be that there is a natural tendency for inequalities in distribution of wealth to increase over time when there is peace. Many people are content to work for someone else, while there are many entrepreneurs seeking to acquire fortunes. If wars take place, a considerable reduction in inequality will usually take place.

The moral is that trying to redistribute wealth by high taxes for decades may not accomplish much and may leave an economy highly unequal in wealth. Countries like France and Germany have wealth Gini coefficients around .7, so they have marginally better wealth distribution than the U.S. and Sweden.[13] Their income distributions are around .3. One should note that Japan which has a less socialistic economy than the U.S. and certainly than the European countries has a wealth coefficient of .55 and a significantly more equal wealth distribution than the socialistic European countries and the U.S. Japan's income Gini is

.25 a very low value.[14] The point is that redistributionary taxation in democratic socialistic countries will tend to produce greater equality of wealth is a superficial view. I believe a laissez-faire economy with strong competition will tend to produce greater equality of wealth.

Greed

Many people believe that people running corporations are consumed by greed and engaged in all kinds of wrongdoing and exploitation. These beliefs were highlighted in recent months by the banking woes. They think that we need to pass regulations and hire government officials to investigate them. However, this is not a good idea for several reasons. First, we are already too regulated. Federal regulations take up an entire wall in a library. Regulations actually give special advantages to lawyers and those who know the regulations. They give people more opportunities for corruption. Second, there will always be some dishonest people in every walk of life. But there is no reason to think that the executives in corporations are any more dishonest than the average member of society. Yet taking extra measures to try to put them in jail and regulate their activities is bound to cause them to pull back and fail to engage in activities that would be productive for our society.

The necessity of competing in free markets to sell goods or services imposes discipline on entrepreneurs. They have to provide goods that people want or the goods or services will not sell. If the products are bad or defective they will not sell or will provide the basis for lawsuits. The Rockefellers, Vanderbilts, and others were successful because they provided good products and services at good prices. They did so better than their competitors and were rewarded well for doing so. That is just what a market system should do to elicit the greatest benefits for society.

The belief that corporate executives are evil is based purely on ideology and propaganda about entrepreneurs of a century ago. There is little evidence of wrongdoing by our corporate leaders. In fact their record is far cleaner than one might reasonably expect. There is a scandal involving indictments and jail time for executives from non-financial corporations from time to time. The Enron affair happened a few years ago. But nearly all the indictments in recent years have involved the banking and financial system which is regulated by government. Much of the problems are caused by bad regulation and bad influences from Congress.

There was political pressure to break up the near monopoly held by Standard Oil. Finally after 13 volumes of testimony and no evidence of wrongdoing by Rockefeller, the Federal Government split Standard Oil into 34 companies in 1911. For over 30 years the Federal Government had sought antitrust action. But by the time Standard Oil was split up, competition had reduced its share to 60% of the refining market. [15] So the competitive environment tended to reduce concentration over time. It doesn't take rocket science to figure out why a laissez-faire market environment will lead to this outcome. If government does not intervene in an economy, but allows laissez-faire conditions with full bore competition in the market, then competition will cause investors to invest in industries that offer higher than average profits. They will make innovations and reduce the dominance of leading companies causing profit rates to fall.

Currently with the credit collapse of September and October 2008, a large part of the blame has to go to members of Congress who have been pushing the banks to make risky loans for the past 15 years. The regulatory agencies that forced mark-to-market accounting to govern bank asset and lending standards may have played a role as well. The Federal Reserve maintained undesirably low interest rates for a number of years which encouraged more inflation in the housing market. Although the public is angry with Wall Street over the affair and no doubt some questionable activities have occurred, it is not evident that what went wrong had anything to do with capitalism. The culprits are really our political representatives and bureaucratic regulators. The main problem was government action by the Federal Reserve and Congress exacerbating the bubble in the housing market. When housing prices started to collapse, some financial institutions were not adequately protected. The housing market is massive and homeowners do not have good financial instruments to hedge the risks of falling home prices as other holders of assets do.

Whether we have our current mixed system or one that is generally laissez-faire, entrepreneurs despite all their protestations about the greatness of free enterprise, are going to try to influence the government to give them advantages over their competitors. When government plays a large role in the economy there are more opportunities for corporate exploitation of the system. There are more agencies to stack with friends of the corporation. Large corporations contribute to political corruption. They influence the government to negatively impact their competitors.

Market Failure

Government intervention in the economy is usually justified by claims that certain markets exhibit market failure. For some reason they are not really sufficiently competitive, so the government must step in and remedy the situation. However, the claims are nearly always based on plausible sounding stories and reasons, but when a careful analysis of the market claimed to exhibit failure is made, the researcher virtually always finds the market works satisfactorily.[16]

The market failure rationale for government intervention is very weak. First, the idea that markets are weak or fail is usually wrongheaded. Many markets are not perfect. But few if any are really so imperfect that government intervention is called for. Profits are seldom excessive. Second, the idea that government bureaucrats know enough to come in and fix a market that has problems is a crazy idea. Because there is so much information individual markets take into account, fixing a market requires virtual omniscience.

U.S. Investment and Economic Growth

During the Twentieth Century government intervened in the U.S. economy because some captains of industry were thought to be acting too unfairly and greedily, and that some industries were oligopolistic, if not almost monopolistic, e.g. oil refining and tobacco. Regulation was supposedly needed. Also many economists and thinkers argued for the idea that many markets are inefficient, that there are market failures, and that government needs to step in and regulate them.

During the Twentieth Century especially after 1909 when the profits tax was instituted, the U.S. Government meddled in the economy in many ways. For much of this period the profits tax has been relatively high. The money supply was contracted during the 1930's. High tariffs were applied for a time. Tax laws have changed many times and the threat of changing them has been constant, causing instability with businesses not knowing how to plan. The unpredictability of FDR's actions was a major problem during the Depression. Burdensome and unnecessary regulations requiring expenditures for unprofitable activity loved by some politician have proliferated. Fortunately, since the tax changes in 1986, the U.S. Federal tax code has been fairly stable with but minor changes.

So about half of our economy is run by various levels of government. There is considerable inefficiency in this sector. The two U.S. industries that are heavily regulated and funded by government--education and health care--are the two industries with major problems. The reason government functions rather poorly is that the incentives are the opposite from those affecting the entrepreneur. Entrepreneurs must be efficient to be successful and have their own money at risk if they fail. The bureaucrat does not have any of his own money at risk. If he is successful, coming in under budget will cause reduction in his next year's budget and his empire will shrink. If he fails, it is just the public's money and he will be rewarded with more money and a larger empire for the next year.

Since the Great Depression, the U.S. has had rather weak investment—no more than about 15 or 16 percent of Gross Domestic Product of which about 10 percent is investment required to replace worn out equipment and plants and about 5 percent investment in housing. This level of investment is rather anemic relative to other developed countries. One of the reasons for poor investment relative to other countries is that *lower profits tax rates in foreign countries attract U.S.*

investment which might have been invested in the U.S. domestic economy had we had low profits taxes.

Businesses generate by far the most savings. Profits taxes take away business savings available for investment. Our tax structure has for decades been designed to heavily tax investment and to promote consumption, more than most developed countries. This surely is an important causal factor for our low saving rate and weak investment. Figure 3-1 shows the investment rates for ten developed or developing countries by decade. Good data is lacking for several of the countries prior to 1960.[17] The countries on the left hand side are more socialistic than the United States and the countries to the right tend to have less government intervention.

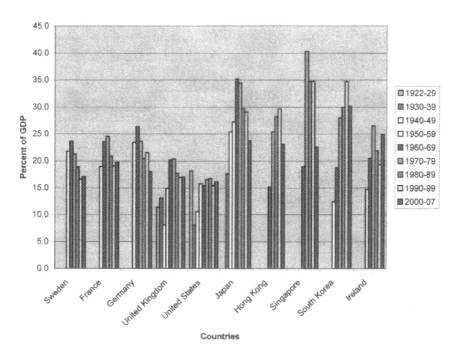

Gross Private Domestic Investment

Figure 3-1 Investment in 10 Developed Countries

We can see from the figure that even Sweden, France, and Germany which have had high taxes, have invested a higher proportion of their production than the U.S. Germany and Japan raised their corporate taxes in the 1970's which no doubt partially caused a decline in investment. Ireland lowered its rate for some manufacturing corporations to 10 percent in 1980 and attracted considerable foreign investment. In 2002 it lowered the corporate tax rate to 12.5 percent generally, producing increased investment. It is noteworthy that countries with the strongest economic growth, Japan and the Asian tigers have high rates of investment.

During the post-World War II period the U.S. experienced some of the best economic growth in its history. But the growth is relatively anemic when compared to Japan and the Asian tigers over a significant part of the period. Average per capita annual per decade growth rates are shown in Figure 3-2.[18]

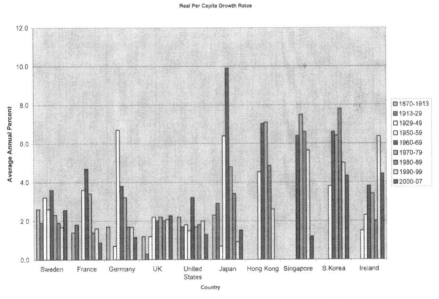

Figure 3-2 Economic Growth by Periods for 10 Economies

In Figure 3-2 data is missing for some countries in the earlier periods. We see that the U.S. has maintained per capita growth rates averaging about 2 percent for the entire period. At 2% annual growth it takes 35 years to double per capita personal real incomes. At 7% annual growth rates typical of Japan and the Asian tigers only 10 years are needed to double real per capita incomes.

Germany had a very high growth rate during the 1950's when production in key economic areas was not subject to corporate taxes and there were other ways to avoid taxes. Japan's growth was very high in the 1950's and 1960's when profits taxes were lower and some taxes were avoidable. One can note that after Ireland drastically lowered its profit rate for foreign manufacturers in 1980 and for all industries after 2002 it had high growth rates. Hong Kong, Singapore, and South Korea have shown high growth rates since the 1960's.

Move Toward Laissez-Faire

The evidence that bureaucrats waste resources and do a poor job most of the time is overwhelming. Unfortunately, when there is a problem with the economy, the left places the blame on the capitalist half and the big, greedy, exploitative corporations. In reality most of the blame should be placed on the socialist half—on the havoc government wreaks on the smooth operation of the economy. Instead of increasing the government role in the economy which only makes perceived problems worse, we should be moving back in the opposite direction. If we free up our markets by reducing government regulation and taxation, we will see a better functioning of the markets and more productivity, more economic growth, and a higher standard of living, especially for the poor. More market competition means that the large corporations may have market share taken from them.

With stronger competition companies must become more aggressive and more willing to hire more labor. When there is strong competition there is less unemployment. Entrepreneurs will take any warm body they can find to train to be productive for their company. On the other hand, when there is significant government involvement in the economy, regulations constrain some or all of the competitors, competition is reduced and the economy is more sluggish. People with the weakest skills struggle with unemployment and poor pay.

I would argue that probably under a laissez-faire regime with low taxes and minimal regulations, the U.S. would have experienced at least 1% greater economic growth per year since about 1909. Consider the implications of this. The 1% increased annual growth compounds annually. So after about 80 years of 1% greater annual growth, the size of the U.S. economy would double its actual size. The average American by 1989 would have had about double the income and wealth he or she had. In fact fewer babies probably would have been aborted and we would have had more people working productively with an even greater GDP. Think of the consequences. World War II probably would not have taken place. Khrushchev in 1956 would not have banged his shoe at the U.N. and claimed "We will bury You." He would have known then that communism was finished. The collapse of Communism in 1989 would have occurred 25 years earlier. The Vietnam War would not have happened. The example of the United States would have convinced more countries to reject socialism and adopt capitalism earlier. The events of recent years undoubtedly would have been much better for us.

If we were to move toward an economy with a much smaller and minimally regulative U.S. Government, the taxes to support government could be about one-quarter of their current level. In a few years greater economic growth would produce greater wealth for nearly everyone. Health care would be cheaper and affordable for nearly everyone. There would not be any taxes on investment like profits taxes. Taxes would be on consumption. There would be stronger competition in the market place. Profits taxes would not take away valuable investment funds from smaller dynamic, well-managed companies hindering them from expanding in their own industry. They would not be hindered from going into other industries to provide better products and to take away market share from large, stodgy corporations. The greater competition would ensure that resources were used more efficiently with less waste and energy supplies would not be of great concern.

Chapter 4—Economic Incentives and the Tax Structure

Government economic rules and regulations determine incentives governing the economic activities of members of a society. The incentives determine whether economic growth is maximal or minimal. If the government is laissez-faire, has adequate property laws, legally enforces property rights and economic contracts, and keeps taxation minimal, people will be responsible for their own welfare and the welfare of their families. If they are industrious and want to acquire wealth, they have the opportunity to do so. If they are only interested in earning enough to have an adequate standard of living and like to spend considerable time in leisure activities, they will have the opportunity to do so.

The Declaration of Independence affirms the right of Americans to seek "life, liberty, and the pursuit of happiness." The idea underlying the U.S. Constitution is a notion that we should have equal political rights and that we should have equal opportunities to engage in activities, follow our goals, and to succeed in life. It is presumed that we have property rights to what we buy or inherit. There are no clauses or phrases implying that everyone should have equal possessions. U.S. law recognizes corporations as persons with legal rights and limits liability of those who own stock in the corporation. Proper incentives in place will tend to reward those who produce the most goods and services desired by members of society. Since many people have a desire to acquire wealth, there is a strong incentive to produce more and make U.S. society as a whole wealthier. Corporations also have incentives to make profits and increase their wealth, because it promotes the welfare of managers, workers, and stockholders.

Government may lay down regulations that change economic incentives. The most important means is through the tax structure. The French Revolution included equality as one of its key goals. It failed largely because of this goal. Nevertheless, socialism became popular in Europe during the Nineteenth Century. In 1880 Germany raised personal tax rates on income to provide for workers' medical and retirement desires. Most European countries followed the trend. As a consequence, personal tax rates in Europe to pay for government services are high. Personal income tax rates are graduated especially in the Scandinavian countries. Although the U.S. has lower tax rates, in general, in terms of the percentage of GDP taken by government, the U.S. is not very far behind European countries.

Although our focus is on profits taxes primarily, a brief look at the effects of personal income taxes is in order. High personal tax rates affect incentives in the workplace. When high earners pay so much in taxes that they are not much better off financially than the average person, they have less incentive to put out extra effort, to produce as much as they might, or to produce better quality work. They will work less and take more leisure time. There is less likelihood of innovations occurring. Most innovations occur as a result of employees finding ways to improve business processes. If there is little reward for innovation, innovations are less likely to occur.

In general we would expect people to make better use of the money they earn than if it is taxed away by government and spent for them. High personal tax rates will give taxpayers incentives to find tax shelters to keep more of the money earned. In the U.S., the Constitution prevents the Federal Government from collecting taxes on municipal bonds. So anyone with high income can shift assets to municipal bonds and reduce his other taxes. When shifted from the private sector to the State or local sector, investment goes to uses that generally do less for improving productivity, long term growth in the economy and personal wealth.

No Free Lunches

Many people seem to think that the economy provides many free lunches. Corporations are supposedly rolling in money and exploiting everybody. So if we raise their taxes, it will not affect economic growth. There is a free lunch. Also the rich have a lot of money. We should increase taxes and give some of the proceeds to the poor. Thus Barack Obama proposed raising the top personal rates by 4% on incomes above $250,000. If there were free lunches and everyone in that income range were happy to contribute another 4%, the extra 4% might generate $80 to $100 billion in additional revenue. However, there isn't a free lunch. If the top Federal rate goes to 39.6%, when State rates are added, the top rate for many will be around 45%. For every extra dollar earned, government will take nearly half. Many upper income people will move some of their assets to municipal bonds. They will seek other tax shelters. As a consequence the taxable income of the group will probably shrink by at least $200 billion causing the net tax increase on the group to be more in the $30 billion range (the average rate on the entire taxable income over $250,000 is about 25%).[1]

When Bill Clinton raised the top rate by 4% in 1993 he claimed it would bring in an extra $50 billion a year for 5 years. As anyone who knows static analysis doesn't work would have predicted, IRS tax data compiled later showed the change netted no more than about $17 billion per year. This lesson should have been learned in 1921. As shown in Figure 4-1, the tax rate on millionaires was raised from 7% to 15% in 1916 and then 77% in 1918 to try to pay off debt from World War I.[2] The tax rate for incomes between $300,000 and $1 million was only 2% less.

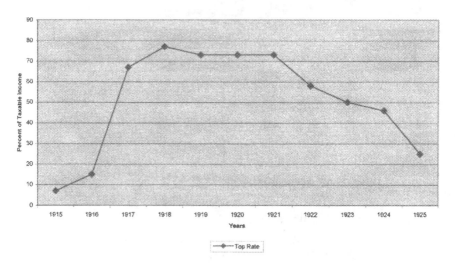

Figure 4-1 Top Personal Income Tax Rates 1915-25

Figure 4-2 shows some of the consequences for revenue collection. The number of millionaire incomes for ten years and the number of incomes above $300,000 for ten years is shown.[3] From 1916 to 1921 the number of tax filers with net incomes over $300,000 dropped to one-sixth its initial number and the number of millionaires fell to one-tenth the 1916 number (from 206 to 21). Although the tax take from the high earners increased from $81 million in 1916 to $244 million in 1919, it fell back to $85 million by 1921 as the number of $300K earners and their combined net income shrank drastically.

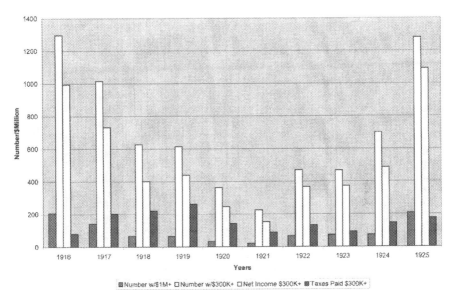

Figure 4-2 Taxpayers with Net Incomes of $300K and $1 Million

Because by 1921 the number of millionaires in the top tax bracket had decreased to one-tenth the number in 1916, the tax take from them did not increase! Figure 4-3 compares 1916 when the top rate was 15%, 1921 when the rate was 73%, and 1925 when the top rate was back down to 25%.[4] The blue and red bars show the number of reported incomes above $1 million and $300,000 respectively. The yellow bars show the income subject to tax for the two brackets. The light blue bars show that the personal income taxes collected from those in the two brackets was about equal. Because the brackets were expanded lowering the level of income taxed, the U.S. government increased the tax take, but not from the two highest brackets. Collections from the top two brackets in 1925 doubled the 1921 take despite the tax rate being one-third the rate from 1921.

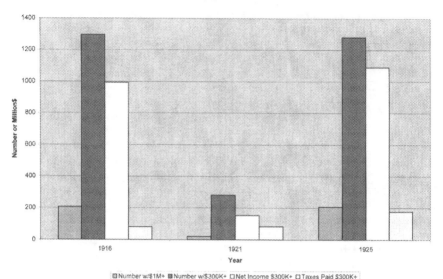

Figure 4-3 Three Years Top Bracket Taxpayers and Revenue

In 1921 Andrew Mellon was called in to be Secretary of the Treasury and figure out the best level for income tax rates. Mellon discussed taxes with rich friends and came to the conclusion that the top rate should not exceed 25% because once it increased beyond that amount, people would start trying to find ways to reduce their tax bill.[5] President Obama's planned top rate is higher than desirable and will push investment into poorer uses reducing productivity and growth and consequently the amount of taxes paid in the long run.

In this book we will focus primarily on profits taxes rather than on personal taxes, but the personal tax rates matter also because they affect the incentives people have to provide services to the economy. Most wealthy people save a considerable part of their income. They either invest the money or borrow and invest through businesses. Savings are more productive and useful if put to work in the private sector. High personal tax rates discourage some productive individuals from working as much since the government takes so much of their earnings. This is a net loss to society. High rates also cause diversion of capital to less productive uses. Investment should go toward the best, most productive, and most efficient uses not usually to the uses which best enable tax avoidance.

Profits Taxes and Incentives

Profits are of course the most important incentive in a productive capitalist economy. Capital is employed if it is expected to bring a return or profit leaving the investor with more in assets than he had before employing it. It makes sense to put the capital to use only if it is expected to provide better returns than could be obtained from less risky interest earned from a bank. Without profits as an incentive we would still be living in a purely agricultural society. There would not be any innovation or economic progress.

Profits have a number of desirable functions. They promote efficiency in the economy. The more efficient companies will earn the largest profits and will be in a better position to invest their greater profits to increase their market share. Profits encourage companies to invest in new factories, equipment, and to fund research. They can fund training for workers to improve productivity. They can give back some of their profits to lower prices for consumers and gain greater market share.

The prospect of greater profits causes innovation. Finding even rather small ways to improve a production process enables a company to reduce costs thereby increasing profits and allowing the company to pay higher wages. Most company leaders want their employees to share in earnings increases. The attitude within companies should not have workers and management at odds, but as members of a team seeking to extract the greatest amount of profit from their industry and share in those profits.

The prospect of profits also gives companies an incentive to investigate opportunities to develop new products and services. There are always problems people would like solved. Usually many people would pay money for a product or service that solved a problem. There are always possibilities of finding new products that would make life easier for people or more enjoyable. If a company can develop a product that solves a problem or fits into some niche that no one else has yet produced, there is an opportunity to make much larger than normal profits while there are few or no competitors and the patent has not expired.

This incentive to make large profits causes innovation and investment where it is most needed or helpful. Of course, the fact that large profits are available in this new field will quickly be noticed by other entrepreneurs who will invest and compete. Some of them may make improvements on the new product. The attraction of new competitors will quickly bring all the investment needed and more. The supply of the product will become more than adequate and the price will fall until the profits are no better than the average profits in the economy. Thus profits fulfill the desirable function of causing investment to quickly go to areas in the economy where it is most needed. Temporarily high profits are attainable. Yet market competition will soon bring profits down to a level where they are no longer excessive, but only average.

Profits give enterprising entrepreneurs opportunities to move into new industries to compete. The profits provide the funds needed to do new things. When adequate profits are available, the prospect of profits promotes strong competition forcing companies to invest more to avoid losing market share. Productivity in the economy is promoted benefiting everyone.

Profits Taxes and Incentives

Those who think that profits taxes are benign fail to see that such taxes affect incentives negatively in several ways. Most industries have large companies with much larger market share than others. Some companies are more profitable because they are well managed and efficient. Others are not nearly as profitable. There are usually economies of scale that bring the greatest efficiency to companies that exceed a certain size beyond which scale no longer produces greater efficiency.

It should be clear that imposing a tax that takes a good half of profits, as the U.S. does, when double taxation of earnings is taken into account, will change the competitive position of different companies in an industry. The stronger more profitable companies will have less retained earnings to fund new investment. They will have less of a competitive advantage over their rivals. Less efficient rivals will survive in an industry longer than if the competition were keener. With less money to invest, gains in productivity and wages will be slower. Competition in the industry will be weaker.

Profits taxes make less money available for research and development to produce new products. Less innovation occurs. New firms often are started with venture capital. A company may also use its retained earnings. Investment is made in new ventures only if savvy investors see a reasonable chance of recouping their investment with a good profit some years down the road. New ventures are not usually profitable immediately or for several years. If, when they do become profitable, the government takes half the profit, the period needed to recover the investment and make a satisfactory return on the investment is extended. Consequently, the existence of profits taxes may discourage some investments that would be made if the taxes did not exist. Some useful innovations may not therefore occur.

Many companies want to keep their dividends up to attract investment in their stock. Consequently the dividends may be a higher percentage of after tax profits than for untaxed profits. The taxes then primarily reduce retained earnings and the primary impact is to reduce money available for investment and actually spent on investment.

When profits taxes are assessed, the taxes are not levied against debt incurred to fund investment projects. Companies can include interest on debt as part of their operating costs. Consequently profits taxes encourage companies to do more funding by borrowing and less from retained earnings. Thus companies will tend to have a higher debt-to-equity ratio than otherwise. Companies having a higher ratio of debt are less sound and potentially more at risk to fail if a recession lasts for a considerable period.

In the late 1980's and early 1990's some very careful studies of the individual and corporate tax structure of major developed countries were conducted.[6] The goal was to find the effective marginal tax rates on capital for each country and determine the relative costs for different economic sectors and different sources of capital for investment. The marginal tax rates are the rates that represent the cost of an additional dollar of capital.

Manufacturing industries require a much heavier investment per worker than do service industries. Figure 4-4 shows the marginal tax rates on the three basic sources of finance for corporations: retained earnings, issue of stock, or debt. These rates were applicable from the last major tax changes in 1986 and are still basically applicable since changes over the past two decades have been minor.[7] Counting double taxation of dividends, the marginal rate on retained earnings was about 60%. Corporations can pay for new investments out of their retained earnings, by issuing new stock, or borrowing the money. Since interest payments are tax deductible, corporations pay very little for the capital they acquire by debt. The tax structure therefore has strong incentives for companies to finance by borrowing and to favor investments in the service and trade sectors over manufacturing. The investments required for starting manufacturing operations are vastly greater than for companies in the service and trade sectors. Since manufacturing corporations require much greater sums for fixed investment, they are more reluctant to finance mostly by debt than service companies and financing will tend to flow more to the service sector and away from manufacturing.

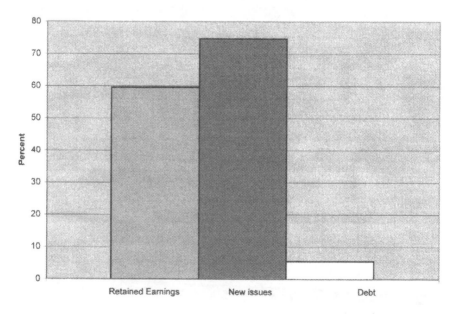

Figure 4-4 Tax Rates by Source of Finance

Thus the structure of profits tax rates provides incentives that cause shifts in investment from the manufacturing sector to other industries. Figure 4-5 shows the marginal rates on manufacturing firms and on commerce and on other industries determined by studies of the 1986 tax code and still basically applicable.[8]. The greater tax rate on manufacturing encourages investment to move from manufacturing to other industries.

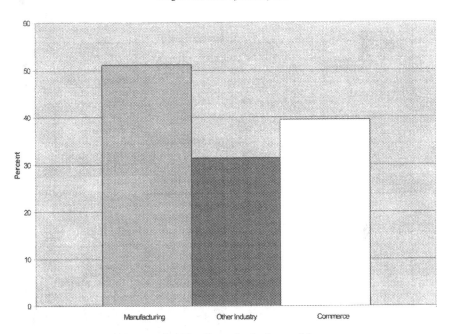

Figure 4-5 Tax Rates by Industrial Sector

Profits taxes also change investment incentives encouraging companies to make their operations more labor intensive rather than investing in more equipment to make workers more productive individually. This slows down gains in productivity and wages.

Taxes that fall more heavily on one sector will shift resources to sectors for which it is lighter. If we separate the U.S. economy into the household sector and the rest into the corporate and non-corporate sectors, the relative marginal tax rates from the 1986 tax code basically still applying today are as in Figure 4-6.[9] U.S. tax statutes shift resources away from the corporate sector to the housing sector. The structure also encourages investment in the non-corporate sector over the corporate sector. Yet the corporate sector's share is at least 61 percent of U.S. employment.[10]

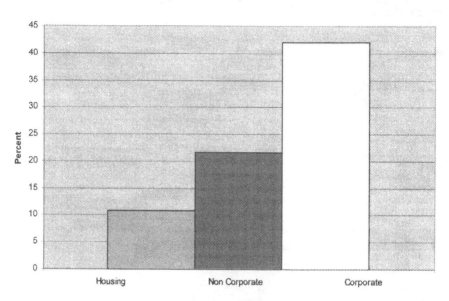

Figure 4-6 Tax Rates by Sector

Section 2—The Goal of Economic Growth

Chapter 5—The Goal of Economic Growth and Resource Availability

The great economic growth produced in developed countries has been a boon to citizens of those countries. Their citizens live far more comfortable lives than they would have a century earlier. A crucial factor in improving standards of living is producing more energy and harnessing it to ease various tasks. Today many people in third world countries live difficult lives. One of the greatest obstacles is the lack of adequate available energy to make their lives easier. With investment in their countries, development of more energy, and good economic growth, their lives could improve greatly. I believe we have a moral obligation not to put obstacles in their way.

Some people who believe we are running out or resources have generated considerable paranoia through the media. They object to seeking economic growth because it requires using more resources. But we need to act rationally. The earth's crust holds a vast amount of minerals of all kinds of which much less than 1% have been mined. [1] There is every reason to think that we will have plenty of resources for most of our needs for centuries or millennia to come. As the easier to mine minerals become more scarce, new technologies are developed to mine minerals buried deeper. Over the centuries the cost of mining minerals has come down in terms of manpower used. There is no good reason to believe that we will not continue to be able to find the minerals we need.

The purpose of cutting profits taxes is to improve economic growth. It is important to consider whether this goal is unattainable by reason of diminishing resources. So we need to take into account reasonable expectations about resource availability. For minerals like iron, copper, silver, gold, etc. there is every reason to expect ample resources for centuries to come.[2] This chapter will examine available energy resources. A rational examination of the situation should indicate resource availability is not a problem and that radical changes are not needed as long as the situation does not change.

Are We Running Out of Resources?

The common belief that we are running out of resources requires examination of the evidence we have. When we have 45 years of proven oil reserves many conclude that we are running out of oil. But it has always been the case that proven crude oil reserves have hovered around 40 years. This is explained by the fact that large oil companies need a window of about 40 years to be comfortable about their future. But they do not have incentives to explore to obtain reserves for a longer period, because they have pressure to maintain profits and dividends and do not want to spend money on exploration before they must. We know that there should be considerable crude oil available from offshore drilling which was banned by Congress until recently. Based on past experience we should expect there is considerable oil left to find.

Figure 5-1 shows U.S. and world energy consumption by source. The U.S. consumes around 100 Quads (Quadrillion BTUs) annually and the world nearly 500 Quads.[3] Crude oil produces the greatest share both of U.S. and world energy consumption. Had reason prevailed years ago, we would have nuclear power contributing a much larger share of power.

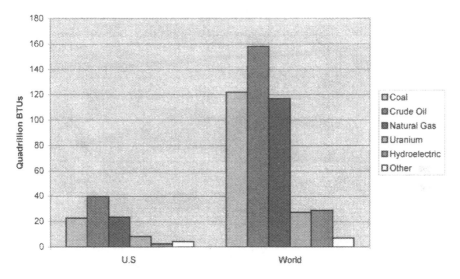

Figure 5-1 Annual Energy Consumption

Fossil Fuels

We do have large deposits of shale oil in Utah, Wyoming, and Colorado. The deposits appear to be the equivalent of nearly 2 trillion barrels of oil, at least half of which should be recoverable.[4] Even if it is not possible to recover nearly all of it, there is enough oil to provide all of the U.S. needs for a 100 years. World oil shale, tar sands, and other heavier harder to process forms amount to over 3 trillion barrels.[5] With world crude oil production at 26 billion barrels per year, if two-thirds of the heavier forms were recoverable, the world would have enough oil at present usage for another 75 years beyond the 45 years reserves of crude. It is highly probable more reserves will be found in the future.

The oil shale is more expensive to recover than current supply. If oil prices rise again as they most surely will, the oil shale will become profitable to recover. Congress must open up the area in Utah, Wyoming, and Colorado for mining oil shale. Many environmentalists oppose it. But it is rational to open up and mine the shale oil. It could provide our needs for many years and give us time to develop other energy sources. It is economically viable to mine oil shale. The oil shale lies underground in a layer that is several hundred feet thick. The soil above it can be stripped off, the oil shale shoveled up and processed and then the soil replaced with the result that the land will simply be lower in elevation by several hundred feet. There is also a feasible method to pump hot steam into the ground and pump the resulting oil out of the ground.

Figure 5-2 is based on the idea that fossil fuels will be the primary fuel for vehicles for many years to come. Transportation uses take about 30% of energy consumption. For the five listed sources of fossil fuels: coal, crude oil, oil shale, tar sands, and natural gas, the bars in Figure 5-2 indicate the number of years each could provide all needs for the U.S. and the world, respectively, for transportation. If we add the bars for fossil fuels for the U.S., available fossil fuels can provide all U.S. transportation needs for at least 650 years. Fossil fuels could provide all world transportation needs for 500 years.

If we moved to providing all energy for electricity and heating from nuclear energy and renewable sources, the bars in the graph for different sources of uranium show the number of years each source could provide all world needs for electricity and heating. The bar for uranium mined from the sea has been greatly shortened to a fraction its proper size for perspective. If only 5% of uranium in the sea were recovered, it would provide all the power needed at present world consumption of electricity and heating for over four thousand years.[6] Breeder reactors can generate as much new fuel as they use providing a vast amount of additional energy. Adding the bars for different uranium sources for the U.S. shows available fuels can provide all U.S. electricity and heating needs for at least 1000 years. Uranium sources could provide for all world electricity and heating needs for 5000 years. Also, because thorium is three times as plentiful as uranium, it could provide all electricity and heat generation for thousands of years, if used in breeder reactors. The thorium bar in the graph is far shorter than its proper length. The graph does not include fusion power. We don't know when fusion will become a viable energy source. It may take a century, but when it does become viable, the available energy from ocean water will be virtually unlimited. The figure shows that we should not have any reason to be concerned about energy resource availability.

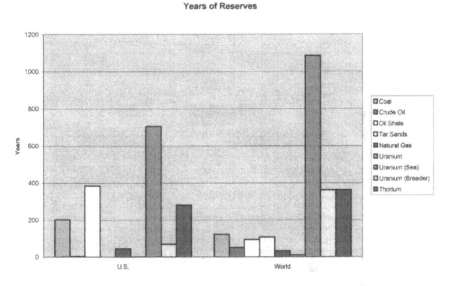

Years of Reserves

Figure 5-2 Future Resource Availability

We have plenty of coal. Coal can be converted to gasoline. Most of the gas that the Germans used during World War II was produced from coal. Since we have an abundance of coal, there is another energy source that would enable the U.S. to produce its own energy without relying much on importing it from abroad. The U.S. has an estimated 275 billion tons of coal reserves which will last for 240 years at present levels of consumption.[7] Coal can be converted to gasoline and if we doubled production and converted the extra production to fuel for transportation, we could eliminate the 4.5 billion barrels of crude oil we import every year. U.S. coal converted to gasoline could provide all U.S. transportation needs for 200 years. Thus the U.S. could be self-sufficient either from oil shale or coal conversion.

The world's reserves recoverable with current mining technology are estimated to be about 900 billion tons, enough to last 170 years at current levels of production.[8] Some geologists believe that world resources are ten times the proven reserves, that is, about 9 trillion tons. There appear to be 3 trillion tons of coal under the North Sea. While not recoverable now, there is every reason to expect the development of gasification techniques will enable exploitation of this vast resource. Even if we ran out of oil, the world would have enough coal to provide fuel for transportation and electricity for hundreds of years without expansion of nuclear power.

Nuclear Power

The most important energy option is nuclear power. Unfortunately the anti-nuclear hysteria promoted by scientifically ignorant U.S. journalists caused the U.S. to stop building nuclear power plants. Nuclear power actually provides the safest form of energy. The U.S. can follow France and reprocess and reuse highly radioactive waste, so there is no storage problem. The U.S. needs to get back to building nuclear power plants to provide for our need for electricity. A considerable reserve of uranium exists (enough for about 135 years at current levels of consumption) and undoubtedly much more is recoverable (believed to be enough for at least 850 years at current levels of consumption). But it is feasible to extract uranium from sea water. There is enough uranium in the sea to satisfy our energy needs for electricity for 100 thousand years.[9] Breeder reactors could provide enough energy for many millenia.[10]

The beauty of nuclear power is that it doesn't emit carbon into the air. This ought to satisfy alarmists paranoid about global warming. Because it will take some time to build nuclear power plants, we have no alternative but to rely heavily on carbon based fuels in the near term.

Environmentalists have been hyping the need to produce alternative sources of energy like wind, solar, and geo-thermal. They want the government to take taxpayer dollars and give them to various groups to develop alternative sources of energy. There are several problems with this idea. First, it is virtually impossible that these sources will ever provide more than a small portion of our energy needs. Government has favored them for years giving tax breaks and subsidies. Yet they have never gotten above two percent of our energy sources. Second, money is much better spent by groups when it is their own money and not money given them by the government. If profits taxes were cut to leave more funds with companies to develop new energy sources, the competition would do far more for developing the energy we need than leaving development decisions in the hands of bureaucrats. Third, wind and solar are intermittent sources. They can only provide supplementary energy. By spending money that would produce much more energy when spent on nuclear or carbon based fuels, considerable resources will be wasted. We should avoid making nearly everyone experience a poorer standard of living than was easily possible.

Crude Oil Dependence and National Security

Obviously importing over 4 billion barrels of crude oil every year (about 70% of our crude oil needs) is not good for our national security. Some of the countries we import from are fairly hostile to us. If there were a war or the importation of oil were disrupted in some way, we could have big problems. It is obviously desirable from a national security standpoint to reduce our dependence on foreign sources of crude oil significantly.

Discussion of the adequacy of our energy resources has shown that by exploiting our shale oil, developing nuclear, more use of natural gas, and converting coal to gasoline we could avoid dependence on foreign oil. Repealing the profits tax and giving permission to do offshore drilling and to develop the oil shale would go a long way toward finding more energy sources and therefore toward energy independence.

Chapter 6—The Goal of Economic Growth and Energy Needs

Aside from the question discussed in Chapter 5 whether the goal of economic growth should be set aside because we might run out of resources, there is the worry about climate change and global warming. Many from the left and in the media believe that the threat of global warming is so serious that there is a pressing need to drastically reduce emissions of carbon dioxide. Because economic growth depends on expanding energy use, any attempt to achieve major reductions in carbon emissions means abandoning the goal of economic growth and accepting a much poorer standard of living.

Is this fear of global warming rational based on the evidence? We need to examine the evidence. When we do so, we will conclude that the evidence does not show there is warrant for taking special measures at this time or in the near future. In fact we couldn't do much to improve the situation even if we committed massive amounts of resources to it. Moreover, an increase in carbon dioxide has benefits. So the goal of cutting profits taxes to improve economic growth and standards of living is desirable, just as was argued in Chapter 5 concerning the question of resource availability.

Why Waste Our Resources?

Of course we should make good efforts to be good stewards of our resources. Relying on capitalist free markets which rewards the most efficient users of resources with the greatest profits is the best way. But there is an irrational obsession and mass hysteria on the part of journalists, politicians, and scientists lacking expertise in climatology, who know very little about the facts. They believe we are in a crisis and that we have to make heroic efforts to move toward alternative fuels and to reduce our carbon emissions.

There are three causes of this mass hysteria. First, some published results from government funded climate simulation models are alarming. Some models have shown global average increases in temperatures of five degrees in less than a century. This might cause some major problems if it were to happen. Over the past 75 years the burning of carbon products for transportation and energy has increased the level of carbon in the atmosphere from about 240 parts per million to nearly 380 ppm.[1] Many people think this has caused global warming and that we should do something to reduce carbon emissions and the amount of carbon products burned.

Second, there is the widespread fear considered in Chapter 6 that we are running out of natural resources. We use a considerable amount of crude oil, natural gas and other resources for our manufacturing and energy needs. Typically there is about 40 years of proven crude oil reserves. Demand is increasing and some people believe we have reached peak oil—that we face declining production in the future because we are running out of oil. As concluded in Chapter 6 this should not be regarded as a serious problem. We have plenty of time to move toward reducing fossil fuel emissions without compromising standards of living. We must rely primarily on fossil fuels for transportation for the foreseeable future, until other sources become viable.

Third, the U.S. imports more than twice as much crude oil as it produces internally. Since some of the countries we buy it from are rather hostile, the national security of the U.S. may be endangered by importing crude oil. For these reasons many want to hastily find alternative fuels and energy sources by heavy government directed investment. This approach will certainly waste considerable amounts of our savings and investment resources. It will significantly reduce productivity gains and gains in our standard of living and leave almost everyone poorer than need be. There is no need to accelerate the process of fossil fuel reduction. With free markets it can happen fairly quickly. If we allow drilling offshore and oil shale mining and build many more nuclear plants, we can allow free markets to take time to reduce fossil fuel use.

Do We Need to Worry About Global Warming?

The claim that there is climate change is about as informative and debatable as someone claiming that the sun will rise tomorrow. There have always been climate change trends on Earth. Some changes have been far more severe than anything we see now. But evaluating the evidence concerning the degree of anticipated climate change is a complex problem. We are probably several decades away from having confidence in predictions.

Having grown up in and currently living in Montana, it definitely seems that winters of late are milder than in my youth. It is also true that bird migration patterns have changed. Many of the migratory birds do not go as far south for the winter as they used to. Robins now hang around during the winter when years ago they didn't appear until March. The glaciers in Glacier Park have been shrinking. However, they have been shrinking for 150 years. The trend started long before human carbon emissions became significant. Although it might seem that this shows there is a long term warming trend, in fact the average summer temperatures in Western Montana including Glacier Park have been unchanged since 1890.[2] Shrinkage in glaciers can occur when there is a cooling trend if there are fewer hours in the winter with the temperatures around 32 degrees and with clouds carrying considerable water vapor.

If it should be true that there are warming trends over certain parts of the earth, that does not mean that there may not be cooling trends on other parts of the earth's surface. And what about the oceans which cover 70 percent of the earth's surface? Measurements of temperatures over the South Pole have often not been available and it is thought that if factored in they might show global cooling. It is quite possible to have global cooling while places in the Northern Hemisphere are experiencing warming trends. The earth's surface is so vast that we should expect statistically to find many places on the earth's surface that have experienced warming trends and others that have experienced cooling trends in recent years. Unfortunately we have many Chicken Little's who cherry pick the data. They find one little piece of data in a small locality and generalize it for the whole earth.

The Historical Evidence

What evidence to we have? There are two kinds of evidence: historical weather measurement data, and data from climate simulation models. First, we should look at historical data. There are a variety of weather measurements. We have weather bureau temperature measurements for well over a century. There are ice cores from ice masses and tree rings that give evidence of weather trends over thousands of years. In the case of temperature measurements the data is skewed towards areas on land that are more densely populated. More recent measurements may be affected by increasing population in cities and better heating. Using the available data to determine an average global temperature leads to different results for different scientists. While there is disagreement among climatologists, we can probably say there is substantial agreement that there has been a very slight warming trend, but not substantial enough to cause alarm. The evidence indicates that there has been an average temperature increase on the earth of less than one degree Fahrenheit over the past 150 years.[3] The main causal factor may be sunspot activity on the sun.

Figure 6-1 makes several points about the historical temperature record. Tree ring and ice core data show that in the 7000 BC to 5000 BC period, temperatures were from 4.5 degrees Fahrenheit to 12.5 degrees Fahrenheit above current levels in parts of the Northern Hemisphere. The straight lines show the lower and upper limits of that period. The other line shows the history of mean temperatures since 1900 in the United States. From 1910 to 1930 mean temperatures in the U.S.

increased by .6 degrees Fahrenheit. They then fell .4 degrees Fahrenheit from 1930 to 1975. From 1975 to 2000 the mean U.S. temperature went up .7 degrees Fahrenheit.[4] The mean global temperature for the Twentieth Century was 57.2 degrees Fahrenheit.[5] In 2008 the mean global temperature was 57.7 degrees Fahrenheit.[6] For the last 10 years the mean temperatures have been flat. We are only half a degree above the average for the previous century, hardly convincing evidence for a major impact from CO_2. The rate of increase during the last quarter of the last century has slowed at least temporarily. It is possible that the trend has changed. But if we ignore the recent flat trend and project the trend from 1975 on, we get the line in the figure showing an increase in the mean temperature of about 2 degrees Fahrenheit above current levels by the end of the Twenty-first Century based on the following evidence.

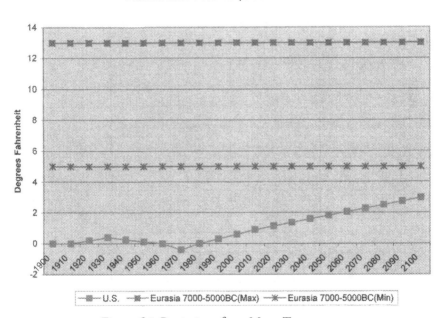

Figure 6-1 Deviations from Mean Temperatures

The United Nations' Intergovernmental Panel on Climate Change (IPCC) publishes surface temperature data that has corrected the original raw data of weather station observations several times in the last dozen years. Every time the data is corrected a greater warming trend is produced.[7] It is clear that some correction must be made to take into account the fact that cities where most of the measurements are made have warmed from better heating and more asphalt and concrete. When the IPCC data is corrected using balloon observations to infer surface temperatures, the trend from 1977 to 2007 is an increase of .23 degrees Fahrenheit per decade or an increase of 2.1 degrees Fahrenheit from 2007 to 2100 if the same trend were maintained from 1975.[8] This is less than projections based on the official corrections that put the decadal increases at .36 degrees Fahrenheit.[9]

Several points need to be made here. First, when the historical evidence is examined the increases in carbon dioxide follow increases in temperature, often by hundreds of years, just the opposite from what should be expected if the global warming hypothesis were true. When the burning of fossil fuels increased greatly after 1930, we should have expected a significant warming of the earth. Instead the earth experienced a cooling trend from 1930 to 1975. We also know that cyclical sunspot activity varies the amount of heat radiated to the earth. This activity undoubtedly swamps the impact of 1/25 th of 1 percent of carbon dioxide in the atmosphere. The addition of carbon dioxide may have had a small impact, but probably not anything we should worry much about.

Second, given the cooling from 1930 to 1975 when fossil fuel emissions increased significantly, and over the last 7 years virtually no increase has occurred, we cannot be sure that the warming trend starting around 1975 will not be reversed for a period of time. Third, before we conclude that fossil fuel emissions pose a serious threat, we need to see a trend that is maintained for considerably more than a 30 year period. Periodically sunspot activity on the sun is suspended for decades as happened during the Seventeenth Century causing the little ice age. It is not inconceivable that this could happen again in the Twenty First Century. Fourth, in view of the fact that there have been many periods when the mean temperatures on earth were at least 4 degrees Fahrenheit greater than they are today, there was probably no ice near the North Pole, and the polar bears survived, it is much too early to panic and start taking extraordinary measures.

We do not yet understand all the phenomena involved with increasing levels of carbon dioxide in the atmosphere. We know that carbon dioxide absorbs more heat from the sun. But there are countervailing effects and we do not know the net effects. More carbon dioxide produces more clouds which reflect sunlight away from the earth causing cooling. Carbon dioxide produces more precipitation which also brings cooling. When we increase the amount of carbon dioxide in the atmosphere a considerable part of the increase is absorbed by the ocean and by plants. Water vapor, another essential part of the life cycle, has much greater warming effects than carbon dioxide. It is quite possible that the net effect on global warming of fossil fuel burning is fairly negligible. We need to learn a lot more before we panic. We will probably be able to make a much better judgment about the effects at least twenty years from now.

Simulation Modeling Results

The media and other alarmists believe simulation models that project higher temperatures by 2100. But simulation models need considerable improvement in their representation of upper atmosphere temperatures, cloud formation, and precipitation before there can be warrant for accepting their results. Some models have produced results suggesting that global mean temperatures will rise by 5 degrees in coming decades. I am all for building models to try to understand the weather. Weather phenomena are very complex and yet worth significant scientific effort to achieve understanding. Climate simulation models should be developed to improve our understanding of weather and climate changes so that we can understand long term trends.

I was a simulation modeler developing discrete event simulation models at Hughes Aircraft Company for 12 years. Those models were different from climate models, but proper modeling procedure is the same. Simulations are creations of the modeler. They will only be good if the modeler understands at least 95% of the phenomena involved and represents it in a good way in the model. The only way to know whether a model is any good is if it gives good predictions that can be tested against measurements of the phenomena being modeled.

Modelers call this validating the model. A scientific model is like a scientific theory. It's predictions must be tested against data that could show it to be false. It must not only have a good fit with past data, but also with future data.

A climate model is only as good as the model creator's understanding of climate phenomena. We still do not have a good understanding of cloud behavior and precipitation. We know that increasing carbon dioxide in the air will cause increasing cloud cover and precipitation. The cloud cover reflects sunlight back from the earth and counters the increased heat absorption from extra carbon dioxide. So modeling these phenomena accurately is vital for deciding the impact of increasing carbon dioxide levels. But climate models do not reflect these phenomena very well and do not simulate upper atmosphere temperatures very well.

We need to have the ability to accurately model all the phenomena that affect climate, before we rely on the climate models for predictions. The accuracy of their predictions over a number of years is essential. Until they give good predictions it is difficult if not impossible to tell where they are wrong. If we are to project climate changes and mean global temperatures forward for 100 years or more, the models need to provide good predictions that can be compared with actual temperature measurements over many places on earth for periods of at least 10 years. It will almost certainly take another couple decades to succeed in designing models that give accurate predictions of global temperatures for ten years to the future. Until we have models that have been validated, we have no idea whether their results should be believed or not. Present modeling results are useful only for the modelers to try to improve their models. They are absolutely worthless for policy decisions. Al Gore and others who accept these results as gospel are showing gross ignorance of proper scientific modeling procedure.

In all the hysteria, the Chicken Littles fail to see that increased carbon dioxide and slightly warmer global temperatures have positive advantages. Carbon dioxide is necessary for plant life and the life cycle. More carbon dioxide causes more plants to grow. It provides more food to support life. It seems that if there is a small increase in global temperatures (although in the last 5 years sunspot activity on the sun has caused some global cooling for all we can tell), it is mostly due to increases in temperature during winter nights in the Northern Hemisphere. This means the main difference is a little more tolerable winters in Siberia and elsewhere and slightly longer growing seasons, both good outcomes. It is really quite nice that Montana winter nights are a little warmer than they used to be.

We know that carbon dioxide at levels of 10,000 parts per million (ppm) will cause a few people to feel nausea. In the past we know that carbon dioxide has gotten up to 6,000 ppm on the earth.[10] At the time this happened, the Arctic ice melted and the polar bears survived. We are a long way from 6,000 ppm, in fact we have gone from about 4% of 6,000 ppm to a little over 6% of that level in the last 75 years. We need much stronger evidence before we alter our lifestyles drastically to try to cut down on carbon emissions.

Figure 6-2 shows the net annual increase in carbon in the atmosphere from burning fossil fuels. Since the oceans and plants are carbon sinks, a considerable absorption of extra carbon dioxide occurs. The figure shows the results of a study of the 1988 to 1992 time period for world wide carbon emissions.[11] The world was divided into three regions with the average annual total emissions shown by the blue bars. There is also a bar for the world totals. The uptake or absorption of part of the emissions produces a net amount of emissions that remain in the atmosphere. Because there is some uncertainty about the amount of uptake for each region, estimates of the maximum and minimum ranges were made. For each region two red bars representing the maximum and minimum net annual emissions for the region are shown. For two regions the minimum net emissions may have been slightly negative.

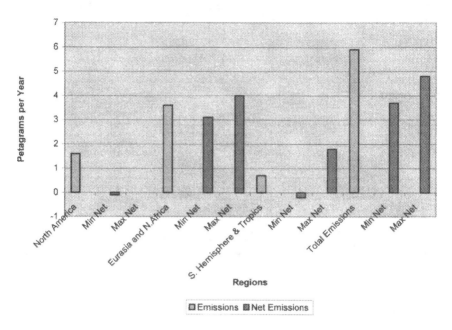

Emissions and Net Emissions

Figure 6-2 Net Fossil Emissions

Environmental alarmists focus on 2.95 Billion metric tons (5.9 petagrams) of carbon that we emit in a year, which is considerable. This was the rate per year for the 1988-1992 period and is a little higher today. Considerable amounts of carbon in the atmosphere are absorbed by plants, trees, and the earth. Indeed North America emitted about 1.6 petagrams and absorbed back at least the same amount. What right do other countries or our own politicians have to ask us to follow the Kyoto accords? The forests in North America have been increasing by about 3% per year which apparently is sufficient along with the ocean to absorb back what we emit. The tropics and Southern Hemisphere emitted about .7 petagrams and absorbed some of it back (-1.1 to .9). For the world as a whole the emissions amounted to 5.9 petagrams per year of which from 1.1 to 2.2 petagrams were absorbed back leaving a net emissions probably above 4 petagrams. It is Europe, Asia, and North Africa which had a net emissions of between 3.2 and 4.1 petagrams per year that are mainly responsible for increased carbon in the atmosphere.

The alarmists also assume that carbon emissions will increase exponentially in the future due to increasing population and greater use per person. However, some thoughtful analysts have concluded that emissions may follow a decline in the rate of increase. If we move to much greater dependence on nuclear power and greater use of natural gas and electric power to power vehicles this is possible. The point is that we can tolerate some increase in carbon dioxide for many years to come. It is also true that we have plenty of fossil fuel to keep us going for a number of years until we develop sources that do not give off carbon dioxide. There is no need to panic. It is likely that a healthy investment in developing fusion as a source of power will produce results eventually. Then with all the deuterium in the sea we would have an energy source good for billions of years at present world consumption.

In conclusion, the evidence does not give us reason to be concerned about climate change. There has always been climate change and at this time there is no reason to think that extreme weather changes are coming. Moreover, there is very little that can be done about it anyway. Draconian measures cutting back on energy would ruin our economy and would accomplish little.

Government Funding of Climate Modeling

Until the 1950's scientific research proceded with some aid supplied by business. Businesses sought help to find applications leading to new viable products. Businesses hired scientists to help in the development of new products as they still do. After profits taxes increased, companies had less money to devote to research. Also the success of the Manhattan Project in World War II in developing the atomic bomb caused U.S. Presidents to believe that government should fund more scientific research. Subsequently the U.S. Government has funded a considerable amount of research. The government funds study of weather including the most prominent climate models.[12]

Unfortunately, funding by government means funding decisions are made by bureaucrats and politicians. The funding then does not depend on conducting sound proper scientific research. It depends

71

rather upon producing frightening results. If the modeling results show drastic changes in the weather that Chicken Little politicians and journalists can hold up as evidence that we need to let them save us from some disaster, then the agencies doing the modeling and the modelers will get more money. On the other hand if their models show that global warming will be minimal, they will probably lose some of their funding. So government funding provides incentives that tend to cause modelers and their supervisors to skew the results toward more extreme and threatening results. This explains part of the reason for the fact that the model results diverge so much from historical measurements of weather data. Further, government left leaning bureaucrats are likely to fund modelers with axes to grind who believe passionately in global warming. If they are funded they will skew results as a consequence of their biases. We need to stop government funding of climate models. It doesn't really cost much to make and run models. Let the climatologists make their studies. Researchers who have a serious interest in understanding climate will find ways to study it on small budgets. Their progress will be as good or better than with government funding. Much of the current funding duplicates other work and is wasteful anyway.

Section 3— Recessions and Economic Policy

Chapter 7—The Business Cycle

A laissez-faire marketplace has a government that does not intervene other than with small taxes to fund the essentials of government and to make regulations which are absolutely necessary. Business cycles should be expected. In good times human psychology tends to become excessively optimistic. Every few years the economy will expand for some time. This boom will end at some point and economic activity will contract in a recession. During the contraction the weakening activity causes businesses to cut back on their workforces because they can't afford to keep everyone busy. They also cut back in investment. So unemployment increases. But after a period of time with weakened activity, spending will increase, new products are often produced, the unemployed will start to be rehired and another boom will begin again. This cycle will repeat itself. The official definition of recessions and expansions is based on statistical estimates of overall economic activity in the economy or Gross Domestic Product—the total goods and services produced in an economy. If the GDP has fallen for two consecutive quarters, a recession is deemed to have occurred. If the GDP continues to increase with no more than one consecutive quarter of negative growth, the economy is considered to be in an expansion cycle or boom.

Figure 7-1 shows the U.S. business cycles since 1919.[1] The date indicates the month the expansion followed by a contraction reached its trough. The blue part of the bar indicates the number of months the U.S. economy was expanding and the red part the length of the following contraction before the next expansion began. The last two bars show averages over the 1919 to 1945 period and over the period from 1945 to the present. During the post-World War II period the expansions have increased in length and the contractions have gotten shorter. For the recent period, the contractions are generally fairly short--on the order of a year, while the expansions typically last for about 5 years.

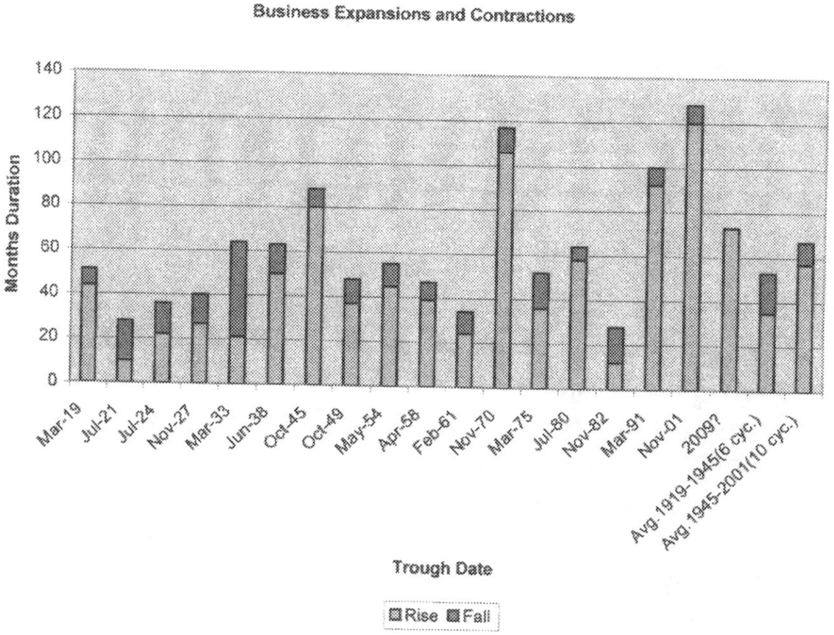

Business Expansions and Contractions

Trough Date

☐ Rise ■ Fall

Figure 7-1 U.S. Business Cycles Ending in Trough since 1919

For 32 business cycles from 1854 to 2001, the expansions averaged 38 months followed by 17 months of recession or depression. The sixteen cycles from 1854 to 1919 had 27 month expansions on average followed by 22 months of decline. The six cycles from 1919 to 1945 averaged expansions of 35 months followed by 18 months of contraction. The ten cycles from 1945 averaged 57 months of expansion followed by an average 10 month downturn. The shortening of contractions is probably due to better government economic policies. Governments know more about what to avoid and know they should expand the money supply.

The business cycle of booms followed by busts can occur in specific sectors of the market, for example the housing sector, and may or may not cause a recession in the overall economy. A very important factor in causing the business boom and bust cycle is the psychology of consumers and businessmen. People generally expect business to be good and their jobs fairly safe. During an expansion people on the whole tend to be optimistic. As time goes on many will tend to engage in more risky investment behavior. Housing and stock market prices are bid up. More borrowing occurs and debt accumulates. As more seek to borrow and the demand for money increases, interest rates rise. At some point the overpriced markets and high interest rates may cause profits to fall or buyers may find they cannot continue to buy at current price levels and interest rates. Fewer first time home buyers are able to qualify for loans. If consumers and businessmen then cut back in spending, a contraction may start.

At this point the mood of consumers and businessmen will be more pessimistic and as businesses cut back and unemployment increases a recession occurs. Less borrowing occurs and interest rates fall. Prices of houses and consumer goods and services will fall as a result of the need to attract more buyers. Eventually the lower prices and low interest rates will cause buying to increase. Optimism will begin to develop and another expansion will begin.

The cycle is self correcting. Expansions will eventually create conditions that will cause a contraction. Recessions or contractions will create conditions that will encourage consumers and businesses to start buying and investing again and the economy will expand. Obviously, the ideal would be a constant gradual increase in production of goods and services that would not be subject to booms and busts. There have been periods in the U.S. of almost ten years of steady expansion, as from 1991 to 2001. But given the role that human psychology plays, the business cycle thus far has always imposed itself.

The government and media can play a role in the business cycle. Governments can cause and greatly exacerbate recessions as well as expansions. The Great Depression became as severe as it did and lasted as long as it did due to government actions. The government passed a very restrictive trade bill that reduced world trade. The Federal Reserve contracted the money supply rather than expanding it. This caused strong deflation. President Hoover believed in balancing the budget and raised taxes. Roosevelt also raised taxes. These measures all worked to make what should have just been a recession into a depression.

Roosevelt was constantly making changes in policy. The uncertainty that this caused was a key factor in prolonging the Depression. Unemployment was still nearly 20% in 1938. The U.S. did not really emerge from the Depression until World War II so it basically lasted for twelve years. It took conscription and enlistment of 10 million men to absorb the 5 million unemployed and to require 5 million men and women to join the workforce to come out of the Depression. Roosevelt introduced large government spending programs and greatly expanded the role of government in the economy, but that accomplished very little in advancing recovery from the Depression. The Roosevelt Administration was very socialistic and created an anti-business environment that surely discouraged businessmen from initiating investment projects. People stayed pessimistic and watched and waited.

Government not only can and often has made recessions worse than they should have been, it also can exacerbate the booms. The excessive boom in the housing market leading up to the recession of 2008 was inflated by government actions. From the early 1990's many members of Congress insisted that banks lower their lending standards to give loans, so people with lower incomes could become homeowners. Fannie Mae and Freddy Mac were encouraged to make shaky loans. As a result for more than a decade many risky loans were made. With loans given readily to buyers of high-end houses as well as low-end houses, prices of houses became inflated. When the bubble finally burst much more pain resulted than ever needed to occur.

The government also in 2007 required banks to hold reserves based on the mark-to-market accounting rule. This forced banks to write down the value of many loans to zero, because they couldn't sell securities, and left many banks with inadequate reserves to make their normal level of loans. The resulting meltdown in the credit markets was a major cause for the severity of the recession. So government has been a major cause of the recession. The mark-to-market accounting rule is generally appropriate, but must have loopholes for banks when markets needed to determine fair market prices collapse.

The spike in oil prices also contributed to the downturn. Gasoline, diesel, and jet fuel became so expensive that some cutbacks in use were necessary. A key cause for the price spike was the behavior of Congressional leaders, who were refusing to open up offshore oilfields to drilling. Crude oil is very inelastic in relation to supply and it appeared to rational people (including of course buyers of crude oil contracts for delivery) that we were about to have a situation where demand was going to outstrip supply.

The media can also increase the severity of recessions and lend strength to expansions. The major media hated George Bush and wanted to see the Republican candidate defeated in 2008. Consequently for much of George W. Bush's second term the media reported on the economy in a much more negative light than was warranted. The economy was in fact growing quite well through 2007, but one would not have known it from most of the mainstream media reports. The media succeeded in helping to cause the recession of 2008 which led to the defeat of the Republican candidate.

On the other side, the media loved Bill Clinton and consistently reported on the economy during Clinton's years in a more glowing fashion than was deserved. For example, the media reported on homelessness during the Reagan Administration but stopped reporting on it during Bill Clinton's presidency. The homelessness hadn't decreased. The constant glowing reporting on the economy probably played a role in extending the expansion beginning in 1991 to last 9 years.

The media of course must report on economic events. We rely on the media for knowledge about the economy. If the economy is bad we need to be able to see the statistics. Similarly, if it is good we need to be able to read about it. But the reporting should be objective and should not reflect liberal biases for or against presidents. During the 2008 election year and before the media had very negative reporting against George Bush. This reporting certainly was a factor in realizing the election of Barack Obama.

Exogenous events may play an important role in causing recessions. The events of 9/11 caused people to stop traveling for a time and caused a recession in 2001 and 2002. If that terrorist attack had not occurred, we might not have had a recession for a few more years. As noted, in 2008 the price of crude oil skyrocketed from speculation about worldwide demand and expectations that demand was going to exceed supply. Government refusal to open up offshore oil drilling played a significant role in this event as well.

Although recessions are psychologically upsetting to many people, causing fears and feelings of insecurity, there are positive effects of downturns. The progress of long term growth requires Schumpeterian creative destruction.[2] Old industries will be replaced by new. Recessions can hasten the process to restructure industries and to produce better long term growth.

In summary, in an economy booms and busts are inevitable. If the economy is left to itself, it will turn around. The trends that led to the recession help to reverse the decline and begin an expansion. The causes of an expansion will tend to eventually produce a recession. Government actions frequently cause a recession to be deeper than necessary and cause expansions to produce a greater bubble than necessary. The media also can play a role in increasing the degree of booms and busts.

Is Government Intervention Needed?

Usually a recession does not seem so bad that many people panic. In due time most people expect the economy to muddle through. But sometimes the perception of a recession will be so bad for many that their psychological response is one of panic. If many people are laid off, many may become concerned about their own jobs. The media may frighten people by its reporting. Many people panic. They cut back to the minimum on purchases and save much more than usual. Businessmen cut back on investment and lay people off. Eventually there will be more spending and the panic will wear off and a recovery will start. But the recession may be quite severe before this happens.

Lord Keynes developed his General Theory as a response to the Great Depression of the 1930's.[3] In a depression many people panic and do not spend as in normal times. Many consumers cut back on spending. Since the response is psychological and may persist for some time, Keynes advocated that the government step in and spend to make up for the inadequate spending by individuals and businesses. In boom times government can run surpluses, collecting more revenue than it spends to prevent expanding so fast that bubbles are created.

The idea of using government fiscal policy to eliminate the business cycle appealed strongly to many economists. It has a strong appeal to politicians who feel a need to be doing something to deal with any perceived problem. The media love activism by Presidents and politicians, so Keynes' prescriptions were applied in virtually every U.S. recession from the 1930's on. In nearly every case the economic stimulus legislation failed to have much detectable impact. Henry Morgenthau, FDR's Secretary of the Treasury admitted that all the spending done to recover from the Depression failed to do anything. [4] After all in 1938, nine years after the 1929 crash, unemployment was still over 19%.

Passing stimulus legislation may do some psychological good. It may cause some people to become more optimistic and to spend a little more. However, the evidence shows that spending stimulus legislation to counter recessions does not really have much impact. Usually the legislation does not get passed until the economy is already emerging from the recession. Secondly, people know the past record of such interventions and many people do not expect them to have a better effect than in the past. Moreover, big spending packages often produce excessive inflation in the long run.

The Keynesian remedy for recessions that uses increased government spending to compensate for weak consumer and business spending and investment is based on assumptions that are questionable. First, it is assumed that when government spends and the money passes into the hands of consumers and business people they will in turn spend it as quickly as under normal circumstances when the economy is growing and people are relatively optimistic. But if people are still pessimistic about the economy from the reporting in the media, they may just put the money in their bank accounts or pay off debt. The money velocity of the added money may stay around zero for awhile. Until the pessimism lifts, businessmen will not borrow the money deposited in banks and put it to work by investing it. This means that the predicted macroeconomic multiplier effects, if they exist, will be limited. Second, the U.S. has abundant resources, but some of them are limited and subject to inelasticity of supply. Government spending may compete for resources with the private sector and may misdirect them into poor uses.

Third, economists assume that money paid for goods or services determines the value of those goods and services. It is hard to avoid making this assumption. However, in fact some investment produces capital that produces much more goods and services over the long term than other investments. Some investments produce much more goods and services and contribute more toward long-term growth than other investments. Thus there are differences in quality that make a difference. Often it is desirable to make distinctions with regard to quality. Certainly the spending and investment of government bureaucrats is of lower quality as contributing toward economic growth than most spending by private enterprises. Bureaucrats waste resources that could have been put to better uses in the private sector to produce more welfare for citizens.

Chapter 8—Does Government Create or Kill Jobs?

The main focus of John Maynard Keynes' General Theory was how to keep economies at full employment by government action.[1] His analytical focus on employment has caused economists and politicians ever since to believe that government can create jobs and that the number of people employed depends upon government policy. The fact of the matter is that government has very little to do with creating jobs. The number of people employed depends primarily on the number of people of working age and how badly they want to earn money or produce goods and services to sell. In fact the main question about jobs is not whether there are jobs for everyone, but *how much someone will pay them*. In general, the more the skills a person has, the better the pay he or she can command.

Almost every U.S. President, it seems, brags about the number of jobs created during his administration. But government only creates government bureaucratic jobs. The problem with government jobs is that every one of them requires collection of taxes every year for funding. When one counts salary, benefits, and costs for a worker's workplace and its maintenance, the average government job surely costs at least $100,000 per year and the money must be collected from taxpayers every year if the job is to be maintained year after year. Government can also spend money for building highways, museums, performing scientific studies, etc. This type of spending will provide temporary jobs for people in the construction industry, but once the roads or bridges have been built it is good to have them, but the jobs do not continue. The spending on the materials used in construction, funds some jobs temporarily to produce the materials, but does not provide permanent jobs. Building a facility for some city or county provides temporary construction jobs. New facilities are unlikely to pay the salaries and costs for their use. The city or county or state will have to assess taxes every year to fund them. The spending projects are often ill conceived and can end up being burdens for the economy tieing up economic resources and local tax resources for years into the future. Those resources are far more beneficial to the public if left to the private sector.

Keynes and his followers advocated government spending to come out of a recession when people have stopped buying and investing. But nothing is said about *where the money for the spending comes from.* Nor are questions asked about whether the money will be spent for greater benefit than if left for individuals in the private sector to spend. When those who love government funding argue for spending projects, they never make comparisons with what would happen if the money were left in the private sector. They operate as if money grows on trees or just magically appears. It may magically appear if government just prints more money to fund projects. The government frequently does just print money to pay for its spending. But when it does, all that can result is inflation—more money chasing the same goods with higher prices resulting for the same goods. Inflation is a hidden tax politicians find convenient to impose because they can spend, while most of the people they represent do not realize they are being taxed through paying higher prices.

An assumption is made that the money spent cycles again through the economy and is multiplied as it is recycled. Keynesian economists think that some of the money is invested as it cycles and recycles through the economy. But how does one know that in a recession people are going to spend money like they do in normal times? When they are concerned about the economy consumers spend less and businessmen do not invest. The velocity of money slows down. There is no guarantee that any investment that is made as a consequence of government spending will be useful for long term growth. Government can and usually does divert spending toward uses that are less helpful for long term growth. For the same quantity of money spent, bureaucrats will almost always produce a poorer quality of result.

Aside from printing money to pay for spending, government can borrow the money from the private sector so that it is no longer available for spending or borrowing by individuals and businesses for projects they had planned. Government may take the money through taxation so that it is no longer available to the private sector. When government diverts money or capital from uses in the private sector, it is always useful to consider what alternative uses it might have had. When individuals save and put their money in a bank, it is available to the banks to lend for investment uses. Businesses may borrow to set up a business, build a factory to produce a new product, buy the equipment needed to hire and put some new workers to work, buy more inventory to sell, replace worn out equipment, etc.

Investment by private firms can provide permanent jobs. In many sectors of the economy even a few thousand dollars can provide a computer, desk, and workspace for a worker. Workers hired must be able to provide a contribution that enhances the operation of the company sufficiently to make paying their salaries worthwhile. As long as a worker is doing enough work to produce comparable revenue or is providing adequate support for revenue earned, the company can continue to employ the worker for many years with small expenditures to maintain the worker's equipment. In manufacturing industries the amount of investment necessary to provide the tools workers need will be much higher--$50,000 or $100,000 or more per worker. But once a company has made the investment required to provide the workspace and tools needed by a worker to be productive, the worker can be employed for many years. This contrasts with government jobs that require spending much more money taxed from the private sector every year and preventing or delaying many permanent private sector jobs from being created. Consequently when government allocates investment, economic growth is reduced along with standards of living over the long term.

The important reason to prefer investments in the private sector is that when the money belongs to the people making the investment they are careful to ensure that the money will be spent in a way that provides very good prospects of providing a return over a long period of time. Investors must have good reason to believe that the new factories or products they are funding should provide good returns for years. There must be good prospects of earning more than could be earned by putting the money out at interest, that is, Keynes' marginal efficiency of capital must equal interest rates. Although private investors do make mistakes, they generally learn to be more prudent in the future. Businessmen with poor judgment go out of business. The private investment therefore generally goes to good, efficient, productive uses. Investment by government bureaucrats and politicians on the other hand is not money belonging to them personally. They do not need to provide returns above the interest rate. There is no risk to them. They will spend in political ways to please special interests and buy votes for the next election.

Jobs

What then is the evidence regarding jobs? The number of people with jobs should depend on how many want to be employed in remunerative work. The question is what wages and salaries will their employers pay them? The upper line in Figure 8-1 plots the U.S. population between 20 and 64 years in age during the post-World War II era.[2] Obviously a considerable portion of women are happy to be housewives and do not seek employment for long periods of their adult lives. The percentage of women in this category declined during the earlier years of the period. Subtracting an appropriate percentage from the mature population for non-participation in the labor force yields the middle line. The lower line plotting the employed civilian population shows fairly close agreement with the middle line. However, some divergence occurs over the last 15 years. It probably results from more people retiring early and from increases in wealth which enable people to take longer periods off during their working years. Note that during this period official unemployment has tended to be minimal and lower than in earlier periods. The stock market increased greatly during the 1990's. This increased many people's wealth and options. The active military is not included here. If it were, there would be even closer agreement of the lines. Obviously there are many factors involved here. Many people in the group are in school. Many work part time jobs. Nevertheless, the figure suggests that employment pretty much depends upon the number of people of working age who want to work.

Workers vs Population

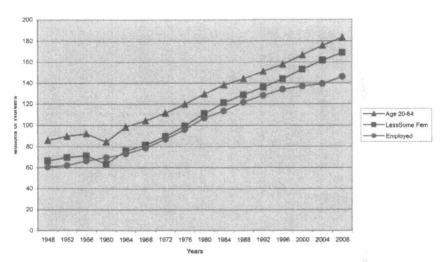

Figure 8-1 Employed Relative to Working Age Population

Keynes rejected the view of Marshall and classical economists who believed that everyone who wanted to work would be employed.[3] Experience since the Great Depression suggests that usually a significant number of people are seeking work and haven't found it. But perhaps they are unwilling to take lower pay or to go into a different field. They may focus only on what they have in the past. Many will be slow to find a different type of job, especially if they are receiving unemployment benefits. There will always be unemployed due to being in between jobs. If many are dependent on somebody hiring them to do a job they have done before, then there will be some dislocations where available jobs of a certain type do not match up with people looking for that type of job.

There are always opportunities for enterprising people. There are always jobs that people will pay money to have done. People however are only employable in so far as they have knowledge and skills. For many jobs the skills necessary can be learned during a short period of training, often on the job.

The marketplace changes over time. There must be creative destruction. If the government steps in to try to maintain certain kinds of jobs for which demand is on the wane, progress and growth can be delayed. We conclude that employment and jobs has very little dependence on government action. The number of government jobs has not increased much in recent years. It isn't the government that produces jobs of any great number. It just funds some temporary private sector jobs.

Chapter 9—The 2008 Panic and Obama's Stimulus Plan

During most of 2008, the economic statistics did not make clear whether the U.S. was in a recession or not. There was a small increase in unemployment early in the year. It was only in October that there were major problems caused largely by tightening of the credit markets. The stock market crashed and unemployment was increasing. By February 2009 it became clear that the recession started around December 2007. Of the ten postwar recessions the average length before hitting the bottom and trending upward has been about 11 months.[1] The length of the recessions was shown by the red shaded portion of the bars in Figure 5-1.

As of this time of writing in May 2009 after 17 months of recession, we are seeing signs that we may have hit the bottom and are beginning to come out. In most of the post-war recessions Congress has passed spending bills intended to counter the recessions. But usually by the time the diagnosis has been made and the spending stimulus has taken several months to get enacted, we have already hit the bottom or are coming out. The Keynesian stimulus spending then either tends to have an inflationary effect or redirects savings from investment in the private sector to a collection of government projects. Left in the private sector the money could fund many permanent jobs rather than poorly conceived projects that may produce some temporary jobs. By directing the savings into uses that do not promote more efficiency, productivity, and long term growth, the stimulus actually slows down recovery and reduces it.

Profits, Consumption, and Investment

Ever since John Maynard Keynes' General Theory was published in 1936, economists have been enamored with the idea that government officials and economists should be able to manage government spending to counteract the business cycle.[2] When a bust or recession occurs they can spend government money and run a deficit to increase the demand for goods. On the other hand, when booms occur, if the government runs a surplus taking in more in taxes and revenue than it spends, then some restraint on the boom will result.

Holding a belief that government should moderate the business cycle of booms and busts involves several assumptions. First, it is assumed that the pain individuals and companies experience in a recession from lost jobs should be eliminated to the extent possible. Presumably everyone will be better off in the long run. But is this the case? It may not be. Schumpeter's observation that capitalism produces considerable creative destruction is apropos. Capitalism encourages innovation. New companies will come forward replacing the old and putting former leading businesses out of business or relegating them to minor roles in the economy. Perhaps for long term growth some bumps in the road are necessary to accomplish needed changes and to advance with the greatest growth. We can not just assume that the best long term growth will occur without the busts. During the past century and a half the average boom or expansion has lasted over 3 years and the average recession a little over a year. In the last 25 years the three expansions have lasted an average of 7 years and the two recessions less than a year. It may very well be that the long term growth is better under such conditions. The pain some feel may be necessary to produce better growth in the long run.

Keynesian economists also argue that the investment generated has a multiplier effect that multiplies the amount spent producing additional benefit.[3] The multiplier effect is based upon those receiving income from government spending it again in return. Those who receive income from them must spend it in turn so that the money spent by government multiplies a number of times. The assumption here is problematic. If consumers in an economy were unaware that a recession is underway and unaware that people they know are being laid off, we would expect them to continue to spend the proportions of income they have in the past. However, when U.S consumers are aware that they are in a recession as they nearly all are, they begin to worry about losing their jobs. They cut back on purchases. Because many panic or believe they need to be prepared for the worst case, much of the money goes into saving. So the government spending will not have the intended effect.

What then is the history of government policymakers trying to mitigate recessions by increased government spending? First, since the U.S. government began trying to increase spending to counter recessions, the success has been quite limited. FDR only prolonged the Depression. He only reduced the ranks of the 5 million unemployed by conscripting and enlisting 10 million for the Armed Services. In most post-WWII U.S. recessions, by the time the recession was diagnosed and Congress succeeded in passing a spending bill, the U.S. was already emerging from the recessions and the extra unnecessary spending probably caused inflation or diverted investment from its best uses to consumption or poor investments, and may have tended to overheat the economy. Moreover, when the spending was government consumption or spending on construction projects many of the projects took several years to implement so that the money did not actually get spent until a recovery had been underway for quite some time.

During recessions of a more recent vintage Congress has made an effort to make transfer payments to individuals. This gives money back directly to persons rather than spending on projects that take time to implement. The assumption is that if the money is given directly to persons, especially low income persons, most of it will be spent immediately. However, money given directly to individuals, who are nearly all aware that we are in a recession, is likely to be saved. Congress takes from private savings and gives the money to individuals who mostly put it back into savings, so that there is little real effect on the economy.

Businesses for their part will not begin to borrow money consumers have put in their savings accounts and to spend it for investment until they see the economy begin to expand. Bank credit problems are also currently preventing many businesses from borrowing. Eliminating profits taxes would help significantly to alleviate this problem.

Given the history of countercyclical measures we are probably better off waiting for the economy to right itself. Otherwise the excessive spending will almost certainly produce considerable inflation. After all when spending and borrowing fall as they do in a recession, interest rates fall and labor costs and resource costs fall providing an environment for increased investment. Spending begins to increase again. Businesses find a need to hire again and an expansion begins.

Many of our leaders in Washington have panicked and are obsessed with spending hundreds of billions of dollars to try to turn the economy around. The proposed Obama budget will add 6.5 trillion to the national debt and raise the ratio of national debt from 40 percent to over 80 percent of GDP by 2019 without even dealing with the funding problems of Social Security and Medicare.[4] It would be wise if our representatives and leaders considered their actions more carefully. The bad news is that economic booms and busts are inevitable in a capitalist economy. But the good news is that they are self correcting and that booms generally last a long time while busts are fairly short (if the government does not exacerbate them as FDR did for the depression). Government actions other than tax cuts generally do more harm than good.

The Prospects for the Current Stimulus Package

Recessions are self-correcting as long as the government does not exacerbate them. Often attempts to reverse them faster than normal may actually slow the process down. Since there are signs that we have probably reached or are close to a bottom, it would be most rational to wait a bit too see what happens. Unfortunately, a huge spending package is likely to have inflationary effects or divert savings into poor investments and slow economic recovery. Politicians want to appear to be doing something, so it is virtually inevitable they will pass some bill that will increase spending. The problem with government stimulus spending is that the type of projects funded generally produce mostly temporary jobs rather than permanent jobs.

Even for spending on infrastructure a long term plan should be followed which does not appear to be the case for Obama's plan. The stimulus is a hodge-podge of projects that make little sense. Without good long term planning the money spent on infrastructure is largely wasted. The long term effect of having our savings spent by government bureaucrats (whose money it is not) rather than by private entities (who are spending their own money) will certainly be poorer long term economic growth.

If we are to do something truly constructive to aid recovery, we should encourage investment. It is increased investment that produces long term productivity and wage growth. If we remove taxes on investment especially the corporate income tax, we would do something very helpful both for the near term and long term economy.

In summary, a moderate amount of additional government spending in a recession may be useful for providing a boost to consumer confidence by trying to show that the government is trying to do something. But large spending bills are counterproductive. If the money is borrowed from the private sector and from our children's future and spent on things that do not provide long term value for future production of goods and services, then the spending is counterproductive and slows future growth. What is beneficial is to pass tax cuts especially tax cuts on profits taxes. Tax cuts have a long term benefit of stimulating investment and economic growth. They also have short term benefits to help come out of a recession. There is every reason to implement them in a recession. They do not force businessmen to invest money, but they do encourage them to invest and they surely will cause additional spending and will accelerate recovery.

Section 4—Let's Eliminate Profits Taxes

Chapter 10—The Corporate Profits Tax

The profits tax was first instituted in 1909 by progressive Republicans on the notion that businesses benefited from government and should pay something as their fair share. The tax was initially very small but was increased significantly by FDR. After WWII it became nearly expropriatory. It has come down since then. For the last twenty years the U.S. Federal Corporate Income Tax rate has been 34 or 35 percent. Many states assess an additional corporate tax usually of 5 to 9 percent. So the average profits tax in the U.S. is over 39 percent.[1] Only Japan is higher and many U.S. states put the combined Federal and State rate at about 41 percent, the highest in the world. One problem with this is that U.S. companies are at a disadvantage in competition with foreign corporations if they pay higher taxes on their profits. A very great problem is that the U.S. is the only country that assesses profits taxes on foreign operations putting U.S. businesses at a competitive disadvantage against foreign competitors. The money does not have to be paid until the money is repatriated.

Many economists and politicians have thought that the profits tax is a benign tax having no deleterious consequences. Apparently, this was Ronald Reagan's belief. When I once claimed it was important to eliminate the profits tax, one of Reagan's economists disagreed with me. Many leaders have thought that it is like a sales tax and is just passed on to consumers. Presumably corporations just raise their prices enough to be able to pay the profits taxes leaving them with the after tax profits they expect.

There are many U.S. industries that have very low concentration. If an industry is composed of small players that are about equally efficient, productive, and profitable, then a profits does act much like a sales tax. However, some unconcentrated industries may have companies with varying profitability. Also, many U.S. industries are fairly highly concentrated. Where there is concentration, some companies are likely to be significantly more profitable than others. Consequently, in some industries some well managed companies will obtain significantly higher profits than poorly managed companies. The profits tax will take a much larger bite out of their earnings and will make expansion in their own industry or other industries more difficult. The profits tax reduces their ability to take market share away from weaker competitors. So the profits tax must weaken competition.

Empirical Evidence—Profits Tax Rates

It is not clear that even most tax charges are passed on, enabling after tax profits to equal profits that would be achieved without the tax. If profits taxes were abolished, no doubt competition would cause some companies to give back some of their extra no longer taxed profits in lower prices to gain market share, but perhaps not all. It is not clear how widespread this practice would be. The companies in some industries might be able to keep the extra profits. The only way to really know is to eliminate or drastically cut the tax and see what happens.

We do know from empirical evidence that low profits taxes benefit economies. When Ireland reduced the manufacturing tax to 10% for foreign investors in 1981 and the trading or corporate profits tax to 12.5 percent in 2003, this move attracted a great amount of investment in Ireland by foreign companies. Many foreign companies built factories. The economy of Ireland which had been quite weak became one of the strongest in the world. Hong Kong had the lowest rate of 17 percent for many years. It had one of the strongest economies for years, until China was to take over and many residents fled with their capital. Swiss corporate taxes have been low and Switzerland has had a very strong business climate as well. After World War II when Japan and Germany were recovering from devastation during the war, their profits taxes were lower than the U.S. and there were many loopholes. Japan and Germany had spectacular post-War recoveries. When they raised the corporate tax rates to U.S. levels they no longer outperformed the U.S.

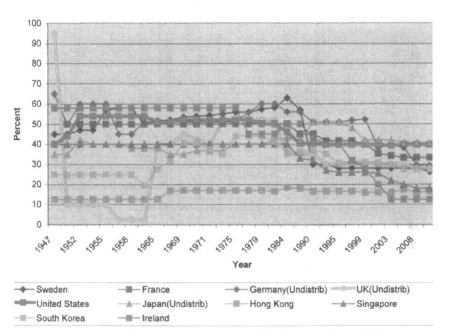

Figure 10-1 International Corporate Tax Rates 1947 to 2009

Figure 10-1 shows corporate tax rates for ten countries.[2] The rates shown are basically the statutory rates for undistributed profits, but not all are strictly comparable. Several countries including Germany, Japan, and the United Kingdom have had a different rate for dividends over a considerable part of the period covered. The German rate includes a business tax paid on income in addition to the corporate tax.

The key rate is really the effective marginal rate which is often higher than the statutory rate. Analysis of the true effective marginal rate is very complex. For the United States during the 1980's the effective marginal rate for undistributed profits was over 60 percent even when federal and state statutory corporate income taxes combined were around 40 percent. The U.S. has higher effective marginal rates primarily because dividends are doubly taxed requiring those who receive dividends to pay personal income taxes on them. During the 1947 to 1954 period, the corporate marginal rate on profits was not Figure 10-1's 55 percent, but may have exceeded 90 percent since most dividends went to the wealthy. The wealthy paid personal taxes at a 90 percent rate and write-offs for depreciation were very inadequate and inflated reported profits.

We note from the figure that countries like Germany and Japan recovering from World War II had corporate tax rates near the U.S. rates, but German manufacturing in core industries did not have to pay corporate taxes. Both Germany and Japan allowed reserves to escape taxes and German businesses engaged in considerable cheating. In the 1970's Germany and Japan raised their rates to be comparable or higher than the U.S. France's rates have been high throughout the period. Sweden has had corporate rates comparable to the U.S., but reduced them considerably since the 1980's. The fast growing Asian tiger Hong Kong has had low tax rates for the entire period. South Korea's rates have been considerably lower at the beginning years and ending years of the period.

Economic Growth

How then do tax rates relate to economic growth? As Figure 10-2 shows, the countries that have had high corporate tax rates have had more stagnant economies.[3] France, Sweden, and Germany (since 1970-2001), are examples of high tax rates and relatively poor performance. Japan had very strong economic growth prior to the 1970's when corporate taxes collected were lower and some income did not get taxed. Germany had high growth in the 1950's when its corporate taxation was lower. When Germany and Japan raised tax rates, growth slowed. Hong Kong has had very strong growth until it became an administration district of China and considerable capital fled. After Ireland lowered its rate for manufacturing corporations in the 1980's to 10 percent and to 12.5 percent for all corporations after 2003 the country produced very strong growth rates. The empirical evidence seems to show substantial correlation between low corporate taxes and strong economic growth.

The economic performance of countries depends upon factors other than corporate taxes as well, but the corporate tax rate is surely a very important factor and the empirical record gives good justification for advocating lowering of the rates, or better yet eliminating them entirely. In recent years the European countries have looked at Ireland's experience and recognized the value of lowering corporate tax rates to stimulate economic growth. Over the last ten years Germany has dropped its corporate tax rate from 50% to 15%(30% including local business taxes). We should view our corporations as engines for providing jobs for people, not as another target for a tax to provide more government revenue. Taxing them weakens their ability to provide more jobs for people.

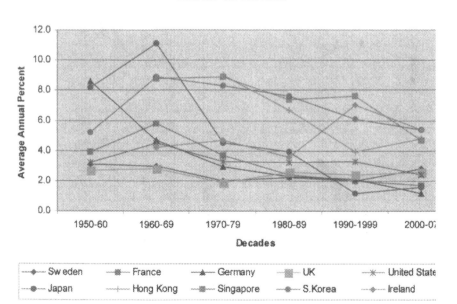

Figure 10-2 Average Growth Rates per Decade for 10 Countries

The General View about Corporate Taxation

Until recently the general view on the economic effects of the corporate income tax is that it is quite benign. Taxing 40% of corporate profits away was thought to have little negative impact on economic growth. There seem to be three main reasons why economists and politicians were not concerned with this practice. First, mainstream macroeconomics assumes that consumers spend in accordance with a propensity to consume function. *Investment is determined by the expected returns to capital invested and the level of consumption because equipment used to produce goods wears out.* Consequently, it is the level of consumption which is the primary determinant of investment. Whether companies have better or worse profits, they will invest an amount which corresponds to their level of sales. They need to maintain output and hence will generate the amount of investment needed to produce that output to handle the level of sales or consumption of their products.

Second, it is thought that corporate income taxes are *passed on to consumers.* Corporations can treat income taxes as one of the costs of doing business and set their prices at a level which will provide them with the return they desire. Since all corporations in an industry must pay income taxes, they will all raise their prices to a level which will provide the same return which they would have expected had income taxes not been imposed. Ronald Reagan believed this and consequently was not concerned when the tax laws of 1982 and 1986 raised corporate taxes back up above their 1981 levels. But unlike the sales tax, the corporate income tax does not fall equally on goods and services produced by different companies. Goods produced by highly profitable companies are taxed heavily and goods produced by companies with losses do not have any tax at all. Removing the tax need not necessarily require the most profitable companies to give back all their extra profits to remain competitive.

Third, some strong economic competitors including Germany and Japan have had nominal corporate rates which are as high or higher than ours, and yet they sustained very strong growth up to the 1970's. It would seem then that our relatively weak investment and economic growth rates cannot be attributed to the corporate income tax and must stem from some other cause.

It is my contention that the adverse consequences of corporate income taxes are far greater than our leaders and economists suppose. The existence of the corporate income tax is a significant factor which has reduced our economic growth for years. It is a main villain in our poor record of investment since WWII. We will first look at why this foolish tax has such an important effect on investment and growth.

Profits Important for Investment

Simple common sense reasoning indicates the importance of profits for determining whether investments will be made. Entrepreneurs and officers of corporations, when considering whether to invest in a new venture or an innovation, will project the prices of the products and expected costs. They will determine expected earnings over a number of years into the future. Having to pay corporate income taxes will reduce the earnings they project and lengthen the period to recoup the cost of the investment. If entrepreneurs do not believe that they can pass the entire costs of income taxes on to consumers, this can determine whether an investment is made. It is quite likely that many entrepreneurs with innovations from the 1980's to the present decided not to implement them, because the risks seemed too great, or the time to recoup the investment seemed too great when tax consequences were taken into account. While many of the potentially most lucrative ventures may still have been funded, many others which are less lucrative, but would have been justified, may not have been tried. As a result, many interesting jobs probably went begging.

Common sense would indicate that over the long run, entrepreneurs are going to look to current profits and the growth of their assets to gauge the expected future profits, if they make an investment. Neo-classical economics assumes that corporations always try to maximize their profits. Corporations with publicly traded stock do have incentives to maximize profits in the short term in order to maintain and raise the value of their stock. We should expect that corporate executives must in the long run seek profits which are adequate to justify making investments.

Corporations which do not follow the practice of investing in view of expected profits, will experience poor returns on their investments and see the value of their stock drop. Keynes argued that investment only occurs if the expected returns over the life of the investment equal the prevailing interest rates.[4] Probably most executives would seek a return several percent above interest rates to cover the extra risk.

Nevertheless some executives may have different goals. Many entrepreneurs may be driven by goals which are not directly profit driven. They may seek to expand their market share and try to become the largest player in their industry. These goals will translate into increased profits eventually. Some businesses operate more defensively and may be quite happy with the status quo. But it is doubtful that they will invest without expecting to see a better return on their investment than if they took the money and invested it in government securities.

If it is true that investment decisions are driven by adequate profits, namely returns on invested capital several percent above long term interest rates, and if entrepreneurs and managers do not expect to be able to pass all of the corporate income taxes on to consumers, some potential investments which would be made under conditions of no corporate taxes, will not be made when the taxes are imposed.

Profits and Interest Rates

The decision to invest is not driven simply by the absolute rate of return. As Keynes noted the decision to invest depends upon the relation between profits and interest rates. When individuals have savings to invest, they will choose between the relative returns on alternative investments taking into account the risks with each. The same also holds true if they plan to borrow the money. Executives must expect to receive a return which sufficiently exceeds the rate they are paying to cover the risks taken. Thus if managers of a company decide to invest to build a new plant and produce a new product, for example, they will generally need to expect to receive a return several percent (three percent has often been used as a rule of thumb) above the rate of return on safe investments like government securities. It is not rational to invest if one expects returns with risk which are less than returns without risk.

A substantial amount of investment must occur just to maintain the business, when the expected returns are poor. Equipment wears out and must be replaced to stay in business. To fail to do so would mean going out of business and losing much of the assets of the business. Given the high tax rates from the 1950's to the 1970's, most of the investment in the U.S. since World War II may have been of this sort.

As is evident from Figures 3-2 and 3-3 in Chapter 3, there is a strong correlation between the amount of investment and profits received. The greater the profits received, the greater the amount of money available to invest to improve competitiveness, future profits, and expand businesses. We would anticipate that executives tend to look to expected profits to continue to invest and that expected profits will tend to follow profits received.

Corporate income taxes reduce profits, because after tax profits are lower than profits without taxes would have been. Corporate taxes in the U.S. have been high since the 1930's. Hence, as was shown by Figure 2-1, U.S. investment is lower than it should be. It tends to be about 15 percent of Gross Domestic Product with 10 percent in capital goods and 5 percent in housing, when other developed economies generally invest more than 20% of GDP. The resulting reduced investment has significantly reduced productivity increases and economic growth throughout the entire post-WWII period. If it has reduced real economic growth by 1% per year on average, then the average employee would be making 60% more per year than he or she currently makes. Over time the impact of the corporate income tax can be immense.

It seems that there are good grounds for believing that the corporate income tax has done significant damage to the U.S. economy. It needs to be reduced drastically. Countries with high growth rates have generally had low corporate income taxes.

The corporate income tax reduces growth in many ways. It has many other adverse effects which are detrimental to individuals. It is the purpose of the following chapters to point out the various pernicious effects in the hope that politicians, policy analysts, and voters, especially lower income voters, can be convinced that, by insisting on onerous corporate income tax rates, they are hurting themselves far more than they are hurting greedy capitalists.

Chapter 11—Profits Taxes and Industry Concentration

Taxes on corporate profits have a number of deleterious consequences. In this chapter we will consider the effects that cause reduced competition and the resulting greater concentration in industries.

The Corporate Profits Tax is an Important Cause of Reduced Competition

I believe that there is evidence suggesting that profits taxes reduce competition and enable large corporations to become larger and more dominant than they might otherwise become. There are some industries which do not have corporations significantly larger or with a much greater share of the market than the rest of their competitors. On the other hand there are industries that have companies that have large market shares. There are companies that are much more efficient, dynamic and profitable than others. If they could keep all of their profits they would have more money to become yet more competitive and productive. They would force weaker competitors to invest more to try to avoid losing market share. With more money available to invest, stronger competition would result. Although in due time competition will reduce profits some, the stronger companies should bring greater efficiency and productivity to their industries. The stronger competition will also bring in strong companies from other industries. Greater competiton will tend to reduce concentration in industries. Consider the graph in Figure 11-1.

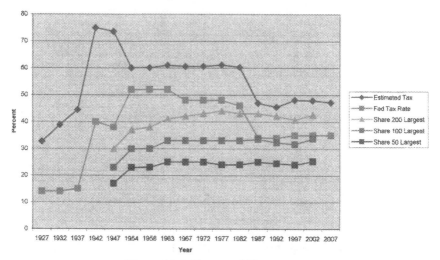

Figure 11-1 Taxes and Concentration

The second line indicates the statutory Federal corporate income tax rate at four or five year intervals from 1927 to 2007.[1] But the true tax rate is higher. First, about 5 percent must be added for state profits taxes that vary from state to state with some as high as 9 percent. Second, there is double taxation of dividends. Prior to the 1960's the top personal rate was 91 percent. The wealthy also received the bulk of the dividends. Many corporations tended to pay about one-third of their profits in dividends. When stockholders pay taxes on the dividends we can figure another 15 to 20 percent in taxes collected by the IRS prior to 1960.

Thirdly, the rules on depreciation can make a considerable difference in profits. If the rules for depreciation accurately reflect the true rates at which assets wear out, then the profits reported are true and the tax rate applied reflects the rate on profits. But if the depreciation schedule is liberal and companies can deduct more than the true depreciation, then they will be able to report smaller profits than the true profits and the official tax rate assessed against the reported profits is less than the actual rate assessed against the real profits. On the other hand, if the depreciation schedule does not allow companies to deduct the full real depreciation, they must report larger profits than they really earned.

The tax rate is then applied to an amount exceeding the real profits and the companies pay a higher rate on their true profits than the official tax rate implies.

Up until the Republicans gained control of Congress in 1952, the allowed depreciation of assets was quite inadequate. Inadequate deductions required companies to report profits that were greater than their real profits and pay a higher tax rate than should have been paid with proper depreciation rules. In 1954 Congress passed changes in the depreciation schedules that greatly liberalized them, so that for some years following, companies were able to deduct more for depreciation than their actual costs, enabling them to pay at a lower rate than the official rate.

The top line in Figure 11-1 represents an attempt to estimate the actual tax rate. To the Federal profits tax rate it adds the average state rate, an estimate of the extra double taxation of dividends and the effect of the IRS depreciation schedules. For the years after 1960 the graphed rate is close to the rates found by careful studies made during the 1980's and early 1990's.[2] For the years prior to 1960 the estimates are very rough although probably a little lower than rates that would be found by careful study. The peak in the rates for the 1940's reflects the inadequate depreciation and very high personal tax rates on dividends paid by individuals in the top tax brackets.

Corporate Profits Taxes and Market Concentration

It is very interesting to take note of the figures for the share of value added in the U.S. economy for the largest 50, 100, and 200 companies as calculated for the Census of Manufacturing taken every five years from 1947 to 2007 (with many results from 2007 not yet available). [4] Because the first such census for which industrial concentration was calculated, was taken in 1947 we do not have good figures for prior years. Figure 11-1 shows percentage of value added for the largest 50 corporations by the lowest line. The next line shows the share of value added in the 100 largest corporations and the middle line shows the share of the largest 200 corporations. It is very interesting to note that the share of value added for the 50 largest corporations in America went from 17 percent up to 23 percent from 1947 to 1954. The share of the next 150 largest increased from 13 to 14 percent during that time bringing the total share of the largest 200 corporations from 30 to 37 percent. Since at this time the burden of profits taxes was very high exceeding 60 percent when all factors are taken into account, there is some empirical evidence suggesting that profits taxes may tend to reduce competition and allow for increased concentration.

It is also interesting to note that while the 1958 shares are very close to the 1954 figures increasing the total for the 200 companies by only 1 percent, there is a significant increase in 1963. From 1958 to 1963 the 50 largest increase their share by 2 percent from 23 to 25 percent and the total for the 100 largest and 200 largest increases by 3 percent up to 33 and 41 percent respectively. In 1962 an investment tax credit was enacted. It was targeted for the large corporations to stimulate investment. Since only the larger companies were able to take advantage of it, it probably explains the significant (3%) increase in share of value added belonging to the largest 100 companies.

The share of the 200 largest continued to increase reaching 44 percent in the Carter Administration in 1977. Since then the share has decreased slightly to 41 percent in 1997, although increasing again slightly to 42.5 percent in 2002. In the 1980's the profits tax rates decreased some and may be a factor in the slight decrease in market share of the 200 largest in recent years.

The fact that a mere 50 firms are responsible for 25 percent of manufactured goods and 200 firms for 43 percent of manufactures in the U.S., seems to indicate there is more concentration in American industry than is desirable. Although the evidence of concentration ratios and corporate tax rates does not prove profits taxes cause reduced competition and increased concentration, it does agree with and suggest such a causal connection exists.

If one examines concentration ratios for different manufacturing industries published by the U.S. Census Bureau's Census of Manufacturing, it is clear that in most industries concentration ratios are quite low.[3] However, when the industry definition is narrowed to certain specific products there are many industries that have only 4 companies generating 40 or 50 percent or more of the value added in the industry. This shows that there is a great amount of competition in the U.S. economy in general, but less in some industries. Of course some industries require very large amounts of investment and are probably only capable of sustaining a few competitors.

Reduced Competition from Profits Taxes

Reduced competition caused by the corporate income tax causes increased concentration in industries. Maintaining competition is important because it keeps prices low for consumers leaving more income available for discretionary spending and saving. Competition also forces businesses to invest more to maintain market share. By investing more they can also reduce costs through achieving greater productivity and higher wages.

When there is reduced competition, on the other hand, companies can charge higher prices. Less competitive companies can obtain larger profits. In spite of achieving higher profits with more money available for investment, the incentive to invest and innovate is actually reduced. Companies do not need to worry as much about competition and innovations which may threaten their market share. They do not need to invest as much. Productivity and wages grow more slowly.

When industries become sufficiently concentrated that a few firms largely control the market, competition is significantly reduced without overt collusion. It simply is not in the interest of any of the players to "rock the boat." By introducing an innovation all the companies would be forced to increase their investment and would have to reduce prices resulting in lower profits for all players. The U.S. auto industry from World War II to the 1970's lacked innovation. The Big Three had improvements they did not implement because they could simply compete on style.

A major effect of the corporate income tax on some industries is that it tends to create barriers to entry against other firms entering the market. By reducing after tax profits, potential new competitors find that they will have a longer horizon in which they can expect to recoup their investment. The longer time frame also increases the risks. New enterprises and innovations are much less likely to enter an industry.

The reduced after tax returns also tend to level the playing field toward mediocrity. More profitable companies have more income which could potentially be used for investment and increasing market share. The large share taken by the government reduces the available funds with which to innovate. Faced with weaker competition, weak companies in an industry can more easily survive and survive for longer with less efficiency and productivity. Their worker wages tend to stagnate.

Mergers and Acquisitions

If there are low returns to capital investments, entrepreneurs find that it is foolish to try to build a large enterprise and become a captain of industry by building new plants and making new products. A better rate of return and a safer one can be expected by investing in government bonds. Or better still, the entrepreneur can leverage his or her investments in real estate where inflation alone will cause appreciation which brings high returns on an investment. It is not accidental that most large fortunes in recent years have been made in real estate. None of these approaches improves worker productivity and builds a basis for greater economic growth.

There is also another way in which entrepreneurs can build large enterprises and become captains of industry without making low return investments in capital goods like new plants and equipment, or in training, or in research and development. They can build large enterprises by takeovers and mergers.

When profits taxes exist, companies that do poorly and lose money are allowed to subtract losses incurred in earlier years from profits earned. If a company loses a significant amount of money, it can become a desirable object for a buyout by another company. The losses can be used to reduce the taxes for the company buying it. There were many bad economic policies instituted from the 1950's to the 1970's including high taxes. Many company executives made bad decisions and some large companies suffered large losses. Consequently, in the post World War II period there have been many mergers and leveraged buyouts often for the purpose of lowering taxes.

There are a number of ways in which the U.S. corporate income tax promotes mergers and acquisitions. First, the U.S. system doubly taxes dividend income. Many corporations must pay dividends to their stockholders to keep the price of their stock from falling. The income tax on profits reduces the money available for payment of dividends. When stockholders receive their dividends they must pay personal income taxes. So the income is taxed twice. In order to avoid double taxation, corporations will tend to retain more earnings than they might otherwise have retained. If also the opportunities for investment in their industry do not seem warranted, because there is overcapacity already, or the expected returns on capital investment are inadequate relative to interest rates, they will need to find other uses for the money. They have several options: they may buy back some of their stock, they may buy real estate or financial assets, or they may buy out competing companies or buy companies in other industries forming conglomerates.

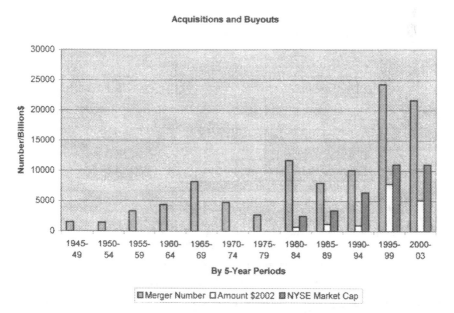

Figure 11-2 Merger Activity in the U.S.

113

Figure 11-2 show the number of mergers and acquisitions in the U.S. over 5 year periods. It includes buying 40 percent or more of another company's stock which usually produces control.[5] For the years since 1980 the figure shows the market value of the acquisitions in constant dollars and the amount relative to the total capitalization of the New York Stock Exchange (NYSE). In recent years the value of the merged or acquired companies has been so great that it has amounted to a large percentage of the capitalization of the NYSE.

During the 1960's buying companies to form conglomerates was all the rage. The economic conditions included high profits taxes and often indifferent returns on investments. Many corporations were awash with cash. Corporate managers thought that conglomerates provided better protection against downturns in their primary industry. If one industry incurred losses, adequate overall profits could still be maintained. The experience with conglomerates has been that the managers whose experience has come from one industry do not know how to manage companies in other industries. The performance of conglomerates was poor.

There seems little doubt that the existence of corporate income taxes had a major effect in encouraging formation of conglomerates in the 1960's and for mergers and acquisitions. During the 1960's the return on capital investments was inadequate.[6] It was more difficult to find productive investments. More earnings were retained but not invested. Corporate income tax rates were very high producing low investment in new plant and equipment.

The corporate income tax encourages profitable corporations to acquire companies with losses to offset profits and reduce income taxes. By having losses, the price of some companies are artificially elevated temporarily because the income tax exists and they are desirable for a write-off. The result is that many more acquisitions are made than might otherwise occur. Companies buy out competitors more readily and increasing concentration in an industry is accelerated. When companies buy other companies for tax purposes rather than for the innate desirability of the company, invested money does not go to its most efficient uses.

The real losers from the reduced competition are the consumers who pay higher prices and have less selection. Workers also suffer since there is less demand for their services. When corporate income taxes are imposed, after tax earnings are reduced. Dividends are also reduced. These consequences result in lower prices for the stock on the stock market. But cheaper stock prices means that it is easier to buy weaker companies. Companies who want to expand their market share in an industry find it easier to buy out weaker competitors and reduce their competition. For their part, the weaker competitors may not resist so strenuously as in an environment in which the government does not take a cut in their profits. The horizon for improving their viability is stretched out. They have less money to invest to become more competitive. All kinds of takeovers and mergers are easier due to reduced stock prices, not just in the same industry.

In the 1980's when returns on capital investments were poor, it was quite predictable that there would be an explosion in takeovers and mergers. When takeovers and mergers are made, improved productivity and improved profits can be obtained. Duplicate middle management and less skilled work can be eliminated through layoffs. Duplicate assets can be sold. Competition in the industry is reduced. If the industry reaches a sufficient level of concentration and oligopolistic structure, higher than normal profits can be obtained by raising prices in a market with diminished supply.

This approach produces greater efficiency. But it reduces competition. It reduces the liklihood of technological innovation because the reduced competition reduces the need for research and development. It also tends to reduce the need for capital investment and training to improve productivity.

Many economists seem to think that the improvement in efficiency is a good thing even if it results in reduced competition. However, it is more important to achieve high competition even if less efficiency accrues. When there is competition there is duplication of effort and less than optimal efficiency in an industry. However, the competition will normally lead to technological advances and greater investment in capital goods which causes many of the competitors to achieve new levels of productivity. Ultimately greater productivity will be achieved than had greater efficiency and less competition occurred.

The Reagan Administration did not seem to mind all the takeovers and mergers taking place. It also encouraged joint ventures by competitors to fight foreign competition. The supposed improvement in efficiency comes at great cost in the long run for consumers and workers. The net result of the increasing concentration means more large enterprises. In the long run, economic stagnation tends to occur from reduced competition. Although in some respects efficiency increases, at the same time large enterprises are by their very nature quite bureaucratic and very inefficient. People who work for them have fewer opportunities to be creative and their jobs tend to be less interesting. Progress is held back.

Auto Industry Example

The U.S. automobile industry offers an example of an industry that became more concentrated than was desirable. As often happens in new industries, the automobile industry started off with hundreds of companies manufacturing cars. But two companies were extremely competitive during the first three decades. Henry Ford developed the Model T which he mass produced at a cost many Americans could afford. General Motors succeeded in combining five different car companies with a strategy for marketing different models for different segments of the car buying marketplace. The dealership network GM set up also was a big advantage. By 1929 Ford had 33% of the market and GM had 37%.[7] One company had 5.3% and the next had 2.7%. The Herfindahl-Hirschman (HH) Index measuring market concentration was over 3700 showing a high market concentration. The Department of Justice begins to investigate industries for excessive concentration when the HH index reaches the 1000 to 1800 range.[8] A market with 10 companies each with 10 percent of the market share would yield an HH index of 1000.

During the 1930's GM increased its market share to 39%, but Ford lost considerable market share falling to 15% while Chrysler surged to 18%. The HH Index using shares of market production fell to about 2800 still showing high market concentration. During this period the profits tax was relatively low. With good competition one should expect the concentration to be reduced over time. After the interruption of World War II, the profits tax had increased to near expropriatory levels. In 1950 and 1960 the HH index was at about 3200. Some excellent car companies like Nash and Studebaker ended up combined in American Motors which survived until 1969. I believe there is reason to think that they might have done much better if there was less government taxation and regulation that reduced the competitiveness of the marketplace and undermined the vitality of smaller companies. With heavy taxation and regulation the HH index increased to 3500 in 1970 and to 4900 in 1980 when GM had 50% of U.S. production. But in the 1980's the Japanese auto manufacturers began building auto manufacturing plants in the United States. The profits tax rates were lowered although still quite high. By 1992 the HH index based on domestic production of cars dropped to about 2900 and by 1999 to 2100 and has remained at the 2100 level through 2007. So we see increased competition after it was necessary to bring in Japanese and German companies to compete with the Big Three automakers.

The Japanese automobile manufacturing industry brings additional insight. Historically it has been more competitive than the U.S. After World War II there were 12 companies competing viciously in Japan. There were low taxes on exports. The result was continuing improvement in quality and continuing innovation just to satisfy the Japanese market. The corporate tax environment, especially for exports, was more benign than in the U.S., where the Big Three competed against each other primarily on styling of the cars. As a consequence Japanese imports made inroads into the American market. By the 1970's Japanese cars were superior in quality to American cars. I would argue that the viability of American car companies would have been much better today if our marketplace had been more competitive after World War II from low or nonexistent corporate taxes and less government regulation. If more automobile companies had survived the 1930's and 1940's, we ought to have seen much more innovation and improvement in American cars than we experienced. Of course, a major problem has been government pressure on GM to settle labor contract disputes too generously during the 1960's and 1970's. The greatest problem for GM is the mountain of legacy costs that have built up. Congress and the Presidents probably should bear as much or more of the blame as the GM executives.

Chapter 12—Profits Taxes and Resource Allocation

The tendency to reduce competition and increase concentration tends also to reduce the perceived need of companies to invest and tends to cause poor allocation of investment. There are also several reasons taxes on profits tend to cause investment money to be allocated in less desirable ways.

Underinvestment in Capital

The most deleterious effect of the corporate income tax is that it causes underinvestment and misallocates resources. There are a number of ways it causes this effect. First, it places investment in capital goods at a disadvantage relative to other types of investments and shifts the mix of investment to *less capital and more labor*. Investment is shifted from its normal pattern into industries which are less capital intensive. Investors will seek industries which, because they depend less on investment, produce better profits. Industries which require heavy capital investments are likely to have inadequate investment and more inadequate profits. This is, no doubt, part of the cause of the shift from manufacturing to service industries in the U.S. Part of the shift may be as a result of natural causes with the development of technology, the information society, and cheaper labor overseas. But a very significant part of the cause may be the corporate income tax. If less capital is invested to improve productivity, wages grow more slowly.

Entrepreneurs and managers have options when they are faced with a need to increase productivity. They can invest in capital goods so that workers can produce more because they have better equipment with which to work, or, they may invest in human capital by providing more and better training, or, they may invest in more innovative methods through research and development. Or, employers can simply hire more workers making the process more labor intensive. In this case, worker productivity does not change. Wage earners maintain lower wages and have more uninteresting jobs when this option is selected. They experience no improvement in their standard of living, since productivity does not increase.

Undoubtedly the shift from a more manufacturing based economy to a primarily service based economy was partly inevitable. However, a study of the incidence of corporate taxes on manufacturing and service industries shows that the burden falls more heavily on manufacturing corporations (see Figure 4-5). Consequently, the corporate income tax is an important cause for the shift from manufacturing to services. During the 1970's many large corporations moved manufacturing operations overseas especially to Asia. Of course, lower labor costs and not having to deal with unions had to be an important factor. But the prospect of lower taxes on their profits must also have been an important factor. Without the high profits taxes no doubt some of the manufacturing operations and perhaps a considerable proportion of them would have remained in the U.S.

Shifting Investment Abroad

Second, high corporate income rates *encourage investment abroad.* More of available funds for investment go to foreign countries and less remains at home. Enterprises find that they are receiving lower returns than would justify investment in new plants and equipment at home because they pay high income taxes. When they also discover that many countries overseas pay lower corporate rates(and labor costs and other costs are lower as well), they may invest in new plants and equipment in the other countries. Some of the shifting is inevitable. But it is not necessary to encourage entrepreneurs to invest in other countries rather than the U.S. simply because the corporate tax rates are too high. Some of the industries which moved to Asia in the 1970's and 1980's might not have moved had corporate income taxes not been in place. They could have achieved satisfactory profits even though labor costs were higher. The labor costs share of operational costs has tended to drop and is less important as a factor driving companies to go abroad.

Investment Shifted to Financial Assets

Third, the existence of high corporate income taxes causes more investment to go to *leveraged financial assets and real estate* rather than to investments which are productive, that is, produce goods and services for consumers. The investment mix is skewed more toward appreciating assets. When returns on capital investments are inadequate because comparable (or better) and safer returns can be earned by other investments, then it is not very rational to build a new plant which is a depreciating asset. If the economy is not in a deflationary cycle, then much better returns can be made in real estate. Since investments in real estate can be leveraged, very high returns can be made. When returns are poor, companies might choose to invest in commercial real estate rather than in plant and equipment. This is a major factor in the real estate boom of the 1980's. Returns on capital investments were poor, especially relative to real interest (see Fig.2-1 and Fig.13-4), yet tax cuts provided plenty of liquidity. The money went into the stock market, financial assets and real estate. The resulting economic growth was largely on paper. Although prices of financial assets and real estate were bid up, little investment was made to improve productivity and to become more competitive internationally. Eventually the paper wealth has to be brought back into line with the real wealth.

Even when returns on capital investments are good, better returns can often be made in real estate. When corporate income taxes are imposed, they cause some investment which might otherwise have gone to capital investments to go into real estate. Hence, the corporate income tax skews investment toward real estate. When we add the personal income tax deduction for mortgage interest, it is no wonder the tax code has caused far too much investment to go into real estate. Real estate investment does nothing to increase productivity. Excessive real estate investment has been a drag on growth in the American economy over the years.

Underinvestment in Human Capital

Fourth, lower investment of returns on capital in productive industries due to taxation of part of the returns, will mean lower R&D, training and wage increases. With less money available to invest, entrepreneurs will not scrimp just on capital goods, but also on other kinds of investment which are often of greater importance in improving productivity. Some desirable research and development projects will not be funded. Less worker training will be offered. The lower growth from lower investment will mean more unemployment. There may be downward pressure on wages. Employers will not need to give wage increases to retain their workforce. They will not feel that they can give increases in view of the pressure on their profits and the need to keep their stockholders happy. On the other hand when investment is strong and the economy is growing, employers find they must compete for workers. They must give back some of their profits in wage increases.

As discussed in the previous chapter, by reducing the rate of return on invested capital, the corporate income tax tends to cause lower investment by decreasing competition. The tendency to decrease competition is a pernicious effect of profits taxes which is generally overlooked.

Financing Shifted to Long Term Debt

Thus far, four very serious consequences of corporate profits taxes have been noted. Profits taxes reduce investment. They cause misallocation of investment. They cause excessive concentration in industries. They cause reduced competition in industries. But there are also several other highly adverse consequences to imposing profits taxes. When these factors are taken into account, one sees that while the corporate income tax may be a most popular tax to punish greedy corporations, it is also the most stupid tax.

First, corporate income taxes *shift the source of financing toward long term debt* in place of direct financing out of retained earnings or by selling stock. The increased use of borrowing to finance projects increases the demand for available funds and therefore also tends to increase interest rates and crowd out some desirable investments. Figure 12-1 shows U.S. tax rates and the ratio of debt to equity for four categories of U.S. companies: large corporations, corporations, non-financial corporations, and manufacturing corporations.[1] The top line shows the top individual income tax rate and the line at about 50 percent during the 1960's and 1970's, the statutory Federal corporate rate. The line below the top line shows an estimate of the actual corporate rate when state taxes, double taxation of dividends, and depreciation allowances are taken into account.

Tax rates increased and were very high during the 1940's and 1950's. High tax rates can have a long term impact encouraging more use of debt. Although the tax rates came down a little in the 1970's and more in the 1980's under Ronald Reagan, the debt-to-equity ratios increased considerably during the 1960's and 1970's, when global competition increased. One line shows debt-to-equity ratios for all U.S. corporations. A second line shows ratios for non-financial corporations and a third line the ratios for manufacturing corporations. A fourth line shows the debt-to-equity ratios for large corporations. Manufacturing corporations that retained operations in the U.S. were forced to take on more debt to remain competitive. Not only did manufacturing corporations take on considerable debt in this period but considerable manufacturing operations were moved overseas at this time. The diagram is consistent with profits taxes tending to be a participating cause for corporations to take on more debt than is desirable.

Taxes and Corporate Debt

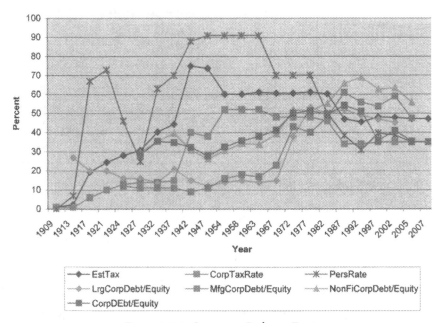

Figure 12-1 Corporate Debt-to-Equity

When a corporate income tax is in place, companies often find that it is preferable to borrow the money for an investment project rather than paying for it out of earnings. The interest paid to borrow the money is deducted from taxes as part of the costs. The earnings on the investment are therefore lower, but taxes do not have to be paid. When the tax rate is around 60% on retained earnings as in the U.S., there are incentives to avoid the tax. *When investments can be made by borrowing, a larger part of earnings can be paid as dividends.* This makes the company's stock more attractive and raises its price.

As noted in recent years the amount of debt relative to stockholder equity has been increasing. Other countries with fairly high corporation tax rates (e.g. Germany and Japan) have historically had *high levels of debt relative to equity.* The U.S. is now much closer to their levels. While financing investments by borrowing is a popular choice and seems to work acceptably well, it is not the approach which is the most sound economically. It exposes companies to greater risk, if there is a recession or depression. Companies in Germany and Japan are less exposed to risk because they are required to have substantial reserves.

Destabilizing Influence

Second, corporate profits taxes have a *destabilizing influence on the business cycle*. When an expansion is occurring, it is spurred on. If a recession occurs, it is accentuated when governments impose corporate income taxes. The explanation for this phenomenon is as follows. Corporations try to maintain their dividends. Whether they are in an expansion or a recession, they are slow to change the dividend payment. When investors see dividends fall they often sell their stock. If corporate leaders reduced dividends in a recession, they would normally see their stock price drop. As a result when profits decrease in a recession, the reduction affects mainly the retained earnings. Consequently, the retained earnings sustain a far greater percentage reduction than profits. The retained earnings may virtually be wiped out. Since new investment comes from retained earnings, a much greater reduction in investment may occur than would occur if profits taxes were not collected. A greater fall in investment will occur than would otherwise occur. But an extra reduction in investment will exacerbate a recession. It is increased investment which is necessary to counter the recession.

On the other hand, in an expansion, retained earnings will experience a greater percentage increase than profits. Because dividends usually are increased only when increases in profits have been sustained over a long period, virtually the entire increase goes to retained earnings. Companies will tend to invest much of the increase. Consequently, large increases in investment will occur during expansions. This causes a greater expansion than normal. The following recession will be a deeper one than normal.

The existence of corporate taxes therefore tends to exacerbate the boom and bust cycle characteristic of free market economies. Often the people hurt worst by boom and bust cycles are the lower income marginal workers who are the first to get laid off when the economy goes sour. Exaggerated boom and bust cycles will tend to cause them to be laid off more frequently and for longer. Thus it is preferable, if a tax must be collected, to use a tax which does not have this tendency. A national sales tax would be a much better approach. Even higher personal income taxes are preferable.

Third, when a tax is on the books, the President and Congress cannot seem to resist making *frequent changes in the tax rates* to influence and "fine tune" the economy in ways they deem desirable. Fortunately from 1986 to 2008 the U.S. had stable tax rates. Only very minor changes were made. This was very beneficial for growth. But our leaders often make frequent changes and cause considerable instability. Corporations must plan many of their major investments over periods of ten years or more. When the government changes tax rates every couple of years, they have difficulty forecasting future returns on their investments. The potential investments are perceived to be more risky. As a consequence, some investments which might otherwise been made are foregone. The problems in planning posed by tax rate instability produces lower investment. An unfortunate side effect of this is that companies also tend to put financial people in charge who look only at the bottom line and do not understand the business and lack vision.

Congressmen and Senators love the corporate profits tax, because having the mere power to increase taxes on business and by making subtle threats, businesses are easily coerced into giving large campaign contributions (especially to Democrats who pose a greater threat to raise business taxes). Raising taxes on business does not cost many votes—corporate executives do not make up a very large proportion of the electorate.

During the Great Depression FDR changed taxes and there was so much uncertainty surrounding government actions and policy, that businessmen did not invest. When an investor does not have any idea what is going to happen and what the returns on a proposed investment are likely to be, he won't invest. If there is uncertainty, investors will just invest in interest bearing securities.

Fourth, the higher concentration and reduced competition enables companies to *raise prices for consumers*. Consumers are forced to put off some purchases they would have made, had prices been lower. Consumers are able to buy fewer goods and services than otherwise and must settle for a lower standard of living. Had consumers been able to retain the money, they would have spent it on other goods and services or invested it and thereby strengthened the economy.

Thus the corporate income tax has additional drawbacks. It raises prices, exacerbates cyclic instability in the business cycle, and promotes corporate financing of investments by borrowing rather than from earnings. It makes companies much more cautious in investing. When these are added to the other adverse consequences: reduced investment, misallocation of investment, excessive concentration and reduced competition in industries, having profits taxes is a policy which ought to be scrapped for the common welfare, especially since the lower income and less skilled workers are harmed the most by the resulting anemic economic growth.

Chapter 13—The Case for Abolishing Profits Taxes

The reasons for abolishing profits taxes are both theoretical and evidential. We will review the main supporting arguments and evidence. Economic phenomena are highly complex. As a result, while I believe the evidence supports my contentions, the case cannot be proven categorically. Some evidence tends to support the case for believing that presumed adverse consequences of profits taxes can be ignored. In the end I believe that the evidence and theoretical arguments are sufficiently weighty that it is wise to eliminate the tax to avoid its problems.

Justifications traditionally given for imposing corporate profits taxes are rather weak. Consumption taxes are far better for generating investment and economic growth than income taxes which tax and discourage investment. In fact the main reason we actually have income taxes is probably their usefulness to politicians. Income taxes generate a large amount of revenue for them to spend. Corporate income taxes mainly antagonize a very small group of voters—corporate executives. So politicians do not have to worry about losing very many votes. More important, corporations have a lot of money they can contribute to political campaign coffers and are a prime source of campaign contributions. By having the threat of raising corporate tax rates in hand, politicians induce corporations to contribute to their campaigns. They are especially useful to Democrats who pose the greatest threat to raise taxes. If anyone is concerned about excessive money spent on politics, they would reduce it considerably by eliminating profits taxes.

The corporate income tax was first levied in 1909 during the Progressive Era at a rate of one percent. In introducing it the purpose of progressive Republicans was to demonstrate that corporations wanted to be good citizens and contribute in response to benefits provided by government. The anti-big business attitudes of the New Deal led to increases up to the 30% range. Profits taxes were greatly increased during WWII to pay for the cost of the war. It was thought to be fair to heavily tax windfall profits. Also, many corporations were supplying goods for the government during the war. Politicians were looking for revenue and it is much easier to raise taxes on thousands of corporate executives representing relatively few votes, than to raise them on millions of taxpayers.

Until recently virtually no one seems to have had any concern about the negative effects of corporate income taxes on the economy. When prescriptions for the economy have been offered, seldom has anyone advocated eliminating corporate income taxes. Republicans normally focus on reducing capital gains. Capital gains reductions are desirable for economic growth and simple fairness and for promoting investment.

Many think that the cost of profits taxes is passed on to consumers and bears a resemblance to a national sales tax. Corporations just raise their prices sufficiently to recover the cost of the profits taxes they pay. Although to be sure, matters are so complex that it is impossible to prove one's case, there are a number of points to be made to show that this claim is very questionable.

Consider an industry that produces a good which can be substituted for another good. Although more expensive, it may provide higher quality. Sellers of the main good in use may be able to pass on the entire tax costs to consumers. However, there may be a price level above which the substitutable good loses market share. If the price needed to offset income taxes is higher, suppliers will find that they cannot afford to increase the price enough to recover their income tax costs. Arguments like this indicate a substantial amount of the costs may not be passed on.

It is necessary to keep in mind that there is considerable variation in profitability of companies in an industry with some much more profitable than others. It would be quite surprising that prices for an entire industry should be exactly the amount to cover profits taxes when some enterprises are highly profitable and efficient and others are unprofitable and inefficient. Due to competition, the more profitable companies may not be in a position to pass on all the tax costs. Since many companies will be unable to do so, it is unlikely that the industry as a whole will pass on all the costs of profits taxes.

The experience of the Asian tigers and Ireland has been that low profits taxes have produced strong economic growth. Ireland by dropping the tax to 10 percent attracted considerable foreign investment. Other European countries took note and have reduced their rates. Germany had rates on the order of 50 percent and has dropped them to 15 percent (30 with local business taxes)..

Summary of Problems with Profits Taxes

The following twelve problems caused by profits taxes were raised in Chapters 10 to 12:
1) Reduced investment and growth over the long term
2) Barriers to entry and reduced competition in some markets
3) Increased concentration in some markets
4) Greater instability in the business cycle
5) Tax rate changes promote instability and hold back investment
6) Increased prices in some markets
7) Reduced wages in some markets
8) Reduced innovation
9) Misallocation of resources
10) Financing shifted toward long term debt
11) Shift of resources from capital intensive to more labor intensive industries e.g manufacturing to service
12) Shift of resources from corporate sector to non-corporate sector and housing

Theoretically, entrepreneurs would expect to have to earn a higher rate of return, if profits taxes are deducted from earnings, and they want to retain the same amount of corporate income that they expect. If the tax cannot be passed on entirely in an industry, it may reduce earnings and act as a barrier to entry for firms wanting to compete in that industry. The reduced competition, resulting also from government regulation, causes increased concentration in industries. When there is less competition and investment, there will be less innovation. If tax payments can be passed on, they will be paid by higher prices or by putting greater pressure on wages.

Corporations try to maintain dividends, retained earnings fluctuate more than usual during a business cycle, which increases volatility in investment. Politicians have difficulty resisting changes in tax rates that induce companies to fill their campaign kitties.

Profits taxes cause investment and resources to be allocated differently than if the taxes were entirely neutral. Consumption taxes are levied at the same percentage against all products so they do not discriminate between products. But profits on products vary from company to company. Some companies pay more taxes on the same products than others do. This situation can cause misallocation of resources.

There are several ways that profits taxes can affect investment decisions. First, investment financed by debt is not taxed. Interest payments are deductible. But investments financed through retained earnings have high tax rates paid, especially because profits are doubly taxed. This causes corporations to finance new investments largely from borrowing and debt rather than from earnings. Carrying higher levels of debt than desirable makes companies less stable. Executives also may invest less due to difficulties in borrowing the amounts they desire. Second, companies can borrow less to produce more by hiring more labor rather than investing more for greater productivity. So investment is shifted toward less capital intensive uses slowing productivity gains and slowing wage growth. Third, profits taxes in the U.S. fall more heavily on corporations than on other companies and on housing. We would expect investment to tend to be shifted toward non-corporate uses and especially toward real estate.

Taxes should be kept neutral so that they don't cause misallocation of resources and provoke inefficiencies. But it is very difficult to achieve this with profits taxes. If there is inflation, creditors are hurt. With inflation profits are also overstated so that the profits tax rate increases. In order to make profits taxes a correct tax on income, depreciation rules must accurately reflect the rates at which structures and equipment wear out. Inventories pose difficulties for accurate accounting of value. In addition there is a certain arbitrariness in how to define corporate income. It is quite difficult to tailor profits taxes to accurately reflect income. These complexities and difficulties provide a good reason by themselves for not imposing the unnecessary profits tax.

In addition to the dozen ways we would expect profits taxes to affect our economy negatively, there is the problem of double taxation. By taxing profits in addition to income of individuals, dividends paid out of profits are taxed first as part of profits and then as dividends in the income of individuals. So not only is capital taxed, some of it is taxed twice. With capital gains and estate taxes it can be taxed a third and fourth time. Some countries try to reduce the impact of double taxation by using one of half-a-dozen methods of integrating the two income taxes. It is not really practical to integrate the taxes fully to avoid any double taxation. Some countries try to reduce the effect by charging lower rates on profits paid out as dividends. The complexity involved is just another reason to eliminate profits taxes.

Theoretical Considerations

In the long run the profits tax must reduce rates of return.[1] It is the after tax rate of return that matters. At the U.S. 35% corporate rate, the before tax profits must be 15.4% over costs to achieve a typical 10% expected rate of profit. We cannot expect all corporations to achieve 15% rates of return. Not all competing corporations will be willing to raise prices enough to obtain 15% returns. When they increase their prices too much, others that try will find their consumers substituting cheaper goods and lose sales. When the after tax returns are less than reasonable, less money is available for investment and the result is permanent reduction in investment, capital, output, productivity, and wages. If this is so, the burden of the tax falls on the corporation shareholders. It also falls on workers in so far as wages do not increase. To the extent that prices are raised to increase profits, it is borne by consumers. We would also expect returns in the non-corporate sector to fall since corporate and non-corporate businesses are competing with each other and should produce comparable profits.

Due to floating exchange rates for the dollar, the U.S. operates as a partially open economy. Eliminating profits taxes should improve expected returns and cause more investment to flow in from abroad. The dollar would rise in value and cause exports to fall somewhat. Profits then would also fall some, but probably not so much as to negate the gains from removing profits taxes. This implies profits taxes cannot be passed on to consumers and must be borne primarily by labor and capital. There would no doubt be some resulting slowdown in productivity growth and wage increases.

Thus far no mention has been made concerning the theoretical aspect of short run consequences for imposing, changing, or removing profits taxes. If classical economic theory holds strictly, there is no shifting of costs in the short run. There are grounds for thinking that this might be the case. If a firm changes its prices to reflect a change in the tax, some of its competitors may not follow suit. There is also a problem of calculation. Taxes are paid on an annual basis. It is difficult for firms to make accurate estimates of the amount of profit that a product will produce for a year and to adjust prices accordingly. It is more difficult yet for a large firm with many products to adjust all the prices to realize a desired after tax profit margin. Firms do not like to raise prices very often. They are sensitive to their customers. So in the short run most prices will tend to be fairly sticky.

The short run classical no shifting scenario depends on assuming perfect competition. With strong competition and possibility of substitution of other products if prices are raised, the degree to which costs can be passed on by higher prices will be limited. Some compensation may be possible by holding down wages. Now we know that some markets are close to being perfectly competitive. However there are some markets that are dominated by a few firms and exhibit imperfect competition.

The utilities industry is regulated by state boards that allow them to earn a reasonable after tax profit for their shareholders and to pass taxes and other costs on to consumers. Leading firms in some industries may set prices which the others follow. In years past U.S.Steel set prices in the steel industry which other steelmakers copied. It seems certain that in many markets and industries it is possible that most profits taxes can be passed on to consumers.

The situation with shifting in the short run is no doubt that profits taxes can be passed on to consumers to some extent. More in some markets than in others. The shifting is only partial. Some of the burden of the profits tax must fall on shareholders and on workers.

Evidence Supporting Need for Reducing Profits Taxes

In Chapter 3 evidence was presented concerning the level of profits taxes, investment, and economic growth for 10 major economies during the post-World War II period. Most of the countries have had profits taxes in the 40 to 50 percent range for considerable periods. The U.S. lowered its rate from 46 percent to 34 percent in 1986 (the total is about 40% when State taxes are included). Some European countries have recognized the value of low profits taxes and reduced them in recent years. Ireland has the rate at 12.5% and Germany at 15% (30% with local business taxes included). Countries are recognizing that low profits taxes are best. The experience of Ireland clearly shows that low profits taxes attract investment. In the United States some States impose profits taxes of as much as 9 percent, while others do not have any profits tax. States that do not have the tax have very good economies and States with high profits taxes tend to have weaker economies.

Hong Kong has always had low income taxes including profits taxes and has had very strong economic growth until the recent takeover by China when many wealthy citizens fled with their capital. In general when profits taxes are lower long-term economic growth is better. Low profits taxes increase earnings and the amount of money available for investment. There does appear to be some correlation between investment and growth and profits. High growth and high investment go hand in hand. The U.S. has tended to grow at about 2% per year per capita, a rather modest growth. U.S. investment is generally around 15% of GDP, which is lower than the investment rate for the other countries. The evidence is not conclusive, however.

Another possible indicator of the consequence of profits taxes is the effect on business fixed investment. As profits taxes increase we would expect some decrease in business investment, since increased before tax returns are sought and more potential investment plans may no longer appear promising. Figure 13-1 shows the ratio of U.S. corporate fixed investment to gross domestic product by the lowest line and to corporate product by the top line.[2] The ratio of business fixed investment to gross domestic product is shown by the middle line. The graphs show that fixed investment as a percentage of GDP increased slightly in the U.S. over investment when profits taxes were lower before World War II. There has been some increase after the 1950's as investment tax credits, accelerated depreciation, and rate reductions were added so that the effective tax rate is lower. So perhaps the investment record gives some support to belief that lower profits taxes encourage investment.

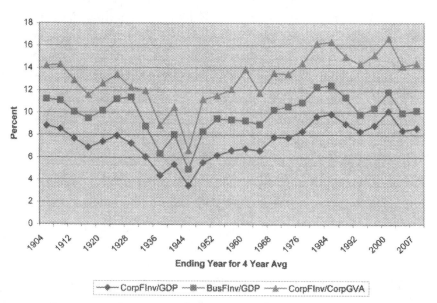

Figure 13-1 Corporate and Business Fixed Investment 1901-2007

Another item of evidence that might give us a clue about the effect of profits taxes on investment and growth is the trend of the ratio of gross corporate saving to Gross Domestic Product. Figure 13-2 shows the ratio of gross corporate saving (undistributed profits and capital consumption allowances) to corporate product with the top line.[3} The ratio of corporate saving to the product of business and to gross domestic product are shown by the middle and bottom lines respectively. Like the fixed investment in Figure 13-1, Figure 13-2 shows a long term mildly increasing trend. Since basically the profits rates were decreasing after 1954 primarily through liberalized capital consumption allowances, we would expect that the amount of corporate saving might show an increase. In 1986 the 10% investment tax credit was repealed, but reintroduced in 1996. Again since effective profits tax rates have been declining slightly over the last half century, a gradual, slight increase in saving by corporations need not be evidence against the thesis that low or non-existent profits taxes improves investment.

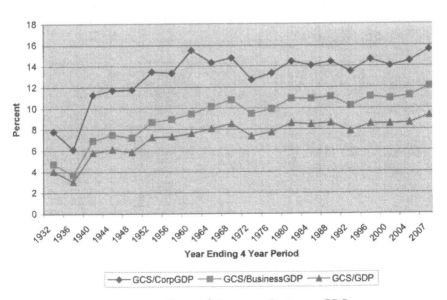

Figure 13-2 Ratio of Corporate Saving to GDP

An increasing ratio of corporate debt to equity would show that profits taxes do tend to cause more borrowing for investment. As shown by Figure 12-1 in Chapter 12, in the 1970's debt-to-equity ratios significantly increased for the categories of large corporations, corporations, non-financial corporations, and manufacturing corporations. From the 1930's to 1954, profits taxes were generally increasing, but corporations resisted reliance on borrowing to invest despite the encouragement of the tax system. During the 1950's and 1960's U.S. corporations were elite. Major competitors like Germany and Japan had been devastated by World War II and needed time to recover capabilities. Considerable saving and investment had occurred in World War II. Also competition was probably reduced by profits taxes, so that there was less need to invest to be competitive. But as global competition heated up by the 1970's, companies needed to invest more to remain competitive. They then found it necessary to invest more and to finance by borrowing. With reductions in profits taxes after 1980, we find that the penalties are less for financing from earnings, and borrowing has plateaued.

In Chapter 4 we pointed out that profits taxes would tend to cause shifting of investment to industries that use less corporate capital. This process has affected the manufacturing industry which has shrunk over the last three decades from about 22% of the U.S. economy to about 11%. Misallocation of resources produces losses of efficiency in the economy. Figure 13-3 shows the share of the U.S. economy held by four major sectors and government, since 1929.[4} Some shrinkage in our manufacturing industry may have been inevitable, but maintenance of our industrial capacity at former levels was surely harmed by taxing away the undistributed profits at high rates and requiring excessive borrowing to fund needed capital intensive investment.

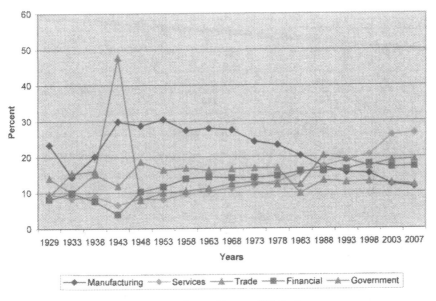

Figure 13-3 Industry Shares of U.S. Economy

Evidence for Believing Profits Taxes are Innocuous

Some of the different types of empirical evidence relevant to the possible benefits of eliminating profits taxes tends to be inconclusive. We would expect after tax rates of return to fall or be level as the profits tax increases. Figure 13-4 shows before tax returns on assets at current cost for non-financial corporations by the top line.[5] It shows after tax returns by the lower line. For the U.S. the after tax rates of return are not better after World War II than they were in 1929 when profits taxes were lower, yet they also show a declining trend even as profits taxes have declined due to investment tax credits and accelerated depreciation.

There are possible mitigating considerations here. During World War II there was a considerable amount of saving and investing to support the war effort. After the war foreign competition was weak. The large amount of war investment no doubt produced very good returns for some years. Nevertheless after tax returns in the 4 to 5 percent range, as they have been recently, are lower than desirable. Nine percent would be quite reasonable. Removing the profits tax would surely help to improve profits and provide better incentives to invest and grow.

Non-Financial Corporations Returns

Figure 13-4 Return on Assets for Non-financial Corporations 1925-2007

One contention has been that the profits tax will tend to shift capital to non-corporate business and housing. We might expect to see the corporate share of product relative to the non-corporate sector and housing to fall over time after higher profits taxes were introduced. However, the corporate share of product has increased modestly in the U.S. over time. In 1929 and through the 1950's the corporate share of product was about 55% and has increased a little to about 60% from the 1980's to the present. The share of product of non-financial corporations has remained around 51% from 1929 on. Three points can be made here. First, the corporate tax has been decreasing gradually since World War II due to decreases in the statutory rate and more liberal depreciation. Second, the corporate form of organization has important advantages since it limits liability of owners and managers. This protection is essential for very large businesses. In particular the 200 largest corporations produce 43% of product. Third, industries like farming for which corporations are not important have declined in share of product.

Conclusion

The conclusion we should reach is that the evidence gives reasonably strong support to the claim that eliminating profits taxes would improve investment and economic growth. The evidence is mixed however. U.S. corporate saving and investment trends seem likely to improve if reductions in effective profits tax rates are implemented.

Chapter 14—The Real Corporatist Big Business Party: The Democrats

The left's mantra that the Republican Party is the party of Big Business has been repeated so frequently that everyone believes it. But shouldn't we follow Jesus' admonition to judge the fruits (actions) rather than what is said? When anyone points a finger at someone else with an accusation, there are three fingers pointing back at the accuser.

We now have a culture in which large corporations and the capitalist system are blamed for most problems. Business corruption is believed to be rampant. Yet Milton Friedman would frequently point out that our system is really about one-half socialist, since governments in the United States spend about 40% of the national income and government regulations mandate at least another 10%. The government involvement in the U.S. economy is massive and I would argue along with Milton Friedman that the economic problems we have are almost entirely caused by government taxation and intervention and not by the market competition. With all the government taxation, regulation, and subsidies there is reduced competition in American industries. A more laissez-faire approach would increase competition, reduce corruption, and cut some of our large corporations down to size. Strong competition is a far better policeman of the marketplace than government regulators who disrupt markets more than they help them.

Regulation also encourages entrepreneurs to depend more on financial manipulation than on producing better products.

Profits Taxes

Few people, even economists, appreciate the deleterious effects of profits taxes on market competition within industries. It is true that most industries in the U.S. are fairly competitive. Yet it is also the case that a mere 50 companies account for 25% of manufactured goods and 200 companies account for 43% of manufactured goods.[1] Many of these companies are multinational corporations that have dominant positions not only in the U.S., but in the global marketplace as well. Because some industries require very heavy investments, there will always be some large companies. But without high profits taxes the competitive landscape would be much more level.

The Republicans did introduce the corporate income tax in 1909 at a very low rate to try to prove corporations were good citizens. But the tax rate was increased greatly during the Depression and World War II by FDR and Truman. During that time and especially right after World War II large American corporations greatly increased their share of manufacturing.

One of the main reasons our multinational corporations moved many of their operations overseas was the lower profits taxes in foreign countries. Low profits taxes attract investment. Ireland lowered its profits taxes to 10% on foreign corporations and immediately attracted much investment and quickly turned its economy around from stagnant to dynamic. Germany has reduced its profits taxes over the past ten years from 50% to 15%.

Profits taxes penalize the best, most efficient companies earning the greatest profits. This reduces their ability to take advantage of better management and operations. Since profits are the best source of money for investment, especially in manufacturing, smaller dynamic companies find it more difficult to move into new industries and expand in their own. Profits taxes act as a barrier to entry. Profits taxes encourage taking on more debt than is desirable.

Regulation

Many on the left seem to think that promoting laissez-faire and strong competition means supporting corporatism and the growth of giant corporations. While the executives of large corporations generally would condemn government regulation of their industry and advocate limited government intervention, in practice they will try to get government to give them special favors and to regulate in ways that cause problems for their competition. In practice, they love to get the protection of government and reduce competitors' competitiveness. They fear the competition of the marketplace. A fierce competitor may come along and "eat their lunch." There are some industries which require large amounts of investment and do not provide enough demand to support more than a few competitors. There are also economies of scale that will tend to favor the growth of companies in a particular industry to a certain appropriate size. However, the libertarian proponent of laissez-faire does not support corporatism and very large corporations. He wants to see them cut down in size by better competition. It is always better to have more smaller companies in strong competition where possible. All too often the large corporations use political maneuvers and political muscle to avoid competition. Laissez-faire will tend to maximize the number of competitiors and keep them relatively small.

If regulations and regulatory agencies are formed to keep companies in line, then there are many untoward consequences that usually result. First, if the government serves notice that it is trying to put people in prison for making too much money, entrepreneurs become discouraged and do not take some of the risks necessary to produce long-term benefit. Second, regulations formed by politicians and bureaucrats often proscribe activities that are not inherently bad. Third, when regulatory agencies are formed, it is usually not long before large corporations with political muscle find ways to get friends on the agency boards and use them do gain favors for themselves and penalties for their competitors. Fourth, unnecessary regulations tend to have fixed costs that fall more heavily on the small producers and have little cost for the large corporations. This may render the small producers less competitive and put them out of business. Fifth, when unnecessary regulations are enacted (and so many of the regulations made by Congress are done just to do something or to make a name for the legislator) there are more opportunities for trial lawyers to perpetrate lawsuits and waste economic resources. Sixth, unnecessary regulations enable well connected people who know the rules to take advantage of them and use them to earn money that does not provide any benefit to society and increases income inequality.

Top corporate executives generally claim that they do not support government regulation and taxation and yet often act quite differently. Many of them, not all, will try to use the government as an ally and fellow competitor against their competition. There is plenty of evidence that corporate elites have strongly supported the imposition of regulations. They support government enforcement of regulations that often simply enforce implicit cartels. They are involved in getting the government to impose quality standards that make it difficult for some of their competitors to stay in business. They seek and get special tax breaks not available to many of their competitors, and the list goes on.

The point is that laissez-faire does not by its nature foster corruption. Rather, strong marketplace competition tends to police and eliminate the corrupt. It is government regulation and taxation that fosters corruption. When government regulates and taxes, resources are wasted on uses that are not productive and most companies that are not parasites become poorer over the long run than they would under a laissez-faire regime.

Reduced competition for large corporations allows them to grow larger than they otherwise would grow. Less competition means they do not have to invest as much to maintain market share. This results in slower productivity and wage growth for their employees. Weakened competition means that large corporations can post good results even when poorly managed. It means that the apparent good performance justifies huge undeserved salaries and bonuses for executives.

The Democratic Party is Really the Party of BIG Business

To sum up the main points above, there are four policies strongly supported by Democrats that are chiefly to blame for the weakened competition in American industries:

1) The corporate profits tax falls particularly hard on manufacturing corporations, which pay at least 50% on their retained earnings (when double taxation of dividends is taken into account). The investment needs of manufacturing corporations are great—too great to allow them to fund mostly by borrowing. The need to rely on retained earnings for investment in new ventures acts as a barrier for smaller, efficient, well run corporations to enter new industries. The dominant corporations in industries are not threatened very seriously by potential competitors entering their industry. They do not have to invest as much to protect their market share from smaller competitors in their own industry, either. If Republicans advocated removing corporate profits taxes, Democrats would strongly resist the action.

2) Government regulatory agencies have been set up with the purpose of keeping companies in line. Democrats believe the public needs protection from predatory corporations. Many think that the marketplace does a poor job of policing corporations and that they must be watched constantly. But bureaucrats always do a poor job of regulating markets. Moreover, the large corporations use their political influence to get people sympathetic to their needs on the regulatory boards. Consequently regulations are made in their favor and to the disadvantage of their smaller competitors. Also, for smaller businesses regulations are generally more costly to implement per item produced and sold and are more likely to go out of business.

3) Many corporate subsidies have been offered to businesses since the 1930's. The subsidies tend to go to the large corporations because they employ many workers especially workers belonging to labor unions. Because Democrats have controlled Congress for much of the past 75 years, they must bear the greatest

responsibility for the subsidies. Many Democrats rail against corporate subsidies, but they have the greatest responsibility for passing most of them. The Republicans of course are not guiltless either. The subsidies should be repealed along with the profits taxes. Since many subsidies are tax breaks, many of the subsidies would be eliminated by eliminating profits taxes. This would be a great boon to smaller, dynamic, more forward looking companies. Figure 14-1 shows the dominance of Congress by Democrats.[2} In the 76 years since FDR came to power, Democrats have controlled both houses of Congress 54 years and the Republicans for 16 years with 6 years of divided control. The positive number of seats plotted above the 0 line in Figure 14-1 shows the number of seats by which a Democratic majority exceeded the seats of the Republicans. The negative plots show the number of seats in a Republican majority. The top varying line shows a party's extra seats in the House of Representatives, the lower varying line a party's extra seats in the Senate. The line at 145 represents the extra seats when a Democratic majority in the House was large enough to override Presidential vetos, that is 2/3 of the seats. The line at 20 shows when Democrats have had 60 votes in the Senate and were able to close off debate and force passage of their agenda in the Senate. For 28 years the Democrats had 3/5 control of the Senate and could ram through anything they wished. The Republicans never had that level of control.

4) Protectionism also reduces competition by limiting competition from foreign competitors. It allows companies to avoid investing and improving. Labor unions want protectionism and many Democrats support them.

I would argue that these policies explain much about our economy. They have caused us to have more very large corporations than we ever would have had, if we had had much stronger free market competition since the 1930's. Since the Democrats have had the most to do with implementing these policies and would squawk long and loud at any advocate for eliminating profits taxes and reducing government regulation, it is the Democratic Party that is really the party of Big

Business. One need merely reflect on the reasons why executives of the largest corporations give most of their political contributions to Democrats to understand this.

U. S. House and Senate Majorities

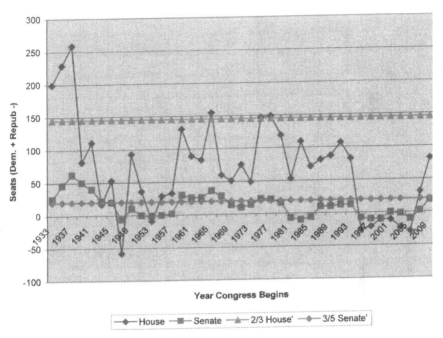

Figure 14-1 Control of Congress 1933 to 2009

Chapter 15—Afterword

Despite those who object to seeking the best short and long term growth for the U.S. economy because they believe that we are running out of resources or causing major climate change from burning fossil fuels, it is highly important to eliminate profits taxes to provide great near term recovery from the 2008/2009 recession and strong long term economic growth. After examining the evidence in Chapter 5 it is clear that we should not be concerned about running out of resources. There are vast amounts of resources available. Also, as documented in Chapter 6, the evidence regarding global warming does not warrant devoting resources to trying to reduce emissions. We should monitor the evidence, if the conclusions should change in coming decades, we can take action when it would be warranted.

The Obama Administration believes that the approach to recovery from the 2008/2009 recession should involve massive Keynesian spending. The proposed spending is so massive that it will add trillions to the National Debt over the next ten years and bring the debt from about 40 percent of GDP to over 80 percent of GDP by 2019.[1] We will be mortgaging the future of our young people. Nothing is done to deal with the unfunded liability of Social Security.

Eliminating the profits tax would produce a major reduction in taxes on investment. The necessary legislation would be simple to pass. Ultimately, the ideal is to switch to consumption taxes which will be a major task to implement. The personal income tax still taxes investment when it taxes capital gains, dividends, and interest. There also is an estate tax. But removing profits taxes would be a very beneficial first step.

It is important not to kill the goose that lays the golden egg. Business which provides jobs and income should be treated like the dairy farmer treats his dairy cows. Their every need is attended to in order to provide a good living. If we do not exercise great care for American business we will "shoot ourselves in the foot" and find ourselves with a poorer standard of living and poorer jobs than need be.

The importance of maintaining strong business to provide jobs also shows the folly of anti-business sentiment. As long as capitalists (and currently a large part of the ownership of capital belongs to pension plans and employees) hold their stock, the capital stock they have part ownership in provides the equipment used by workers to produce goods and services and is a public benefit. Their stock shares are merely deeds to part of it. Taxing income to the corporation reduces its rate of growth and makes the owners of capital including workers and their pensions less wealthy than they otherwise might be.

By reducing the wealth and competitiveness of companies the workers can be harmed as much as owners. Employers can avoid giving raises because the economy is more stagnant and there is a ready labor pool. In a more strongly growing economy with competition for workers and more earnings available, the wages and salaries of workers will go up. Those who are anti-business and believe business exploits workers who want to impose higher corporate taxes, actually end up harming the workers, making them worse off. I conclude the justifications for imposing corporate income taxes are relatively weak.

Positive Developments

One problem discussed for some time is that foreign companies have found ways to avoid paying profits taxes. The remedy proposed was to increase taxes paid by foreign companies to make things fair. However, this would reduce investment in the U.S. economy. A much better approach to equalize domestic and foreign corporations is to eliminate corporation taxes altogether. This approach ensures the position of domestic companies vis-a-vis foreign companies is no longer inferior. It also has the great benefit in promoting investment and economic growth in contrast with the opposite approach of increasing taxes on some corporations and reducing investment and economic growth.

The benefits from eliminating the corporate income tax are not inconsequential. A one percent annual increase in real GDP would result in a 22% increase in GDP over a twenty year period. Comparable increases in personal income would occur as a result.

The greatest benefit from cutting U.S. corporate tax rates will be that other countries will find they must follow suit. This will produce stronger investment and growth in all the countries Stronger growth in global competitors will enhance foreign trade for all. It will provide additional growth for the United States. If not done, the current recession could persist far longer and persist globally as well and produce wars and world instability. Let's decide for policies that will promote worldwide economic growth and worldwide peace.

The benefits to eliminating the corporate profits tax are many:

1) Increased retained earnings provides more funds for investment.
2) There will be increased competition in many industries
3) Concentration in some industries may be reduced
4) More investment will improve economic growth
5) More investment will improve productivity and wages
6) There will be better allocation of resources
7) Finding new energy sources will be accelerated
8) Boom and bust cycles will be moderated to some degree
9) Corporations will use less debt financing and carry less debt
10) There will be more innovation

Although eliminating the profits tax has great benefits for the economy, it may be difficult to eliminate because it is so popular and beloved by Congressmen and Senators. They love it because raising profits tax rates only loses a few votes from corporate executives. By having it available Congress can threaten to raise taxes on corporations encouraging them to offer campaign contributions. Corporations are a good scapegoat to use to rail against and threaten.

Footnotes

Chapter 1

Section 1

Chapter 2

[1] Keynes, John Maynard, The General Theory of Employment, Interest, and Money (New York, Harcourt Brace Jovanovich, 1953), p.135.

[2] Samuelson, Paul, and William Nordhaus, Economics, 12th Ed. (New York: McGraw-Hill, 1985)

[3] Jorgenson, D.W. and J.A,. Stephenson, "Investment Behavior in U.S. Manufacturing, 1947-1960," Econometrica, Vol. 35, No. 2 (April 1967), pp. 169-220. This paper argues for maximizing returns and capital gains as the driving factor behind investment by large corporations based on analys of relevant data.

[4] Keynes, p. 135.

[5] Bureau of Economic Analysis, NIPA Tables 1.7.5, 1.14.

[6] Economic Report of the President 2008, Tables B-60, B-73.

[7] Bureau of Economic Analysis, NIPA Tables 1.7.5, 6.19A-D.

[8] Bureau of Economic Analysis, NIPA Tables 6.7, 6.14A-D, 6.19A-D.

[9] U.S. Bureau of the Census, Current Population Reports, P60-235.

[10] Bureau of Economic Analysis, NIPA Tables; U.N. National Accounts; IMF Data.

Chapter 3

[1] OECD 2009: Society at a Glance, p.4.

[2] U.S. Census Bureau, Current Population Reports, P60-235.

[3] U.S. Census Bureau, Current Population Reports, P60-232.

[4] U.S. Census Bureau, Current Population Reports, P60-191.

[5] ibid.

[6] U.S. Census Bureau, Current Population Reports, P60-204, p. 3.

[7] Forbes Magazine, Mar. 11, 2009.

[8] Pope, Clayne, "Inequality in the 19th Century," in Engerman, Stanley and Robert Gallman, Cambridge Economic History of the United States (Cambridge: Cambridge University Press, 1996), pp. 109-142.

[9] ibid.

[10] Davies, James B., et al. "World Distribution of Household Wealth," Dec. 2006, World Bank, Table 10.

[11] ibid.

[12] Klevmerken, N.Anders, "The Distribution of Wealth in Sweden: Trends and Driving Factors," Working Paper 2006:4, Upsala University. Statistics are quoted from Statistics Sweden.

[13] Davies, James B., et al. "World Distribution," Table 10; OECD 2009: Society at a Glance, p.4.

[14] ibid.

[15] Folsom, Burton W. Jr., The Myth of the Robber Barons (Herndon, Virginia: Young America's Foundation, 1991), pp. 83-100.

[16] Spulber, Daniel F. ed. Famous Fables of Economics (Oxford: Blackwell, 2002). Debunks claims of market failure in virus industries.

[17] Calculated from U.N. National Accounts statistics and various publications for the 10 nations including the U.S. Bureau of Economic Analysis.

[18] Rostow, W.W., The World Economy (Austin, Texas: University of Texas Press, 1978); U.S. Bureau of Economic Analysis NIPA Tables; and U.N. National Accounts statistics and various publications.

Chapter 4

[1] IRS Statistics on Income, 2009.

[2] www.taxfoundation.org/files/federalindividualratehistory.

[3] Mellon, Andrew, Taxation: The People's Business (New York: MacMillan Co, 1924), pp. 97, 191,193, 221. Statistical Abstract of the United States, 1928.

[4] Mellon, ibid.

[5] ibid.

[6] Jorgenson, Dale W. and Landau, Ralph, eds. Tax Reform and the Cost of Capital, and King, Mervyn, and Don Fullerton, The Taxation of Income from Capital: A Comparative Study of the United States, United Kingdom, Sweden, and West Germany (Chicago: University of Chicago Press, 1984).

[7] Jorgenson and Landau, Tax Reform, "United States" Fullerton, Don, and Karayannis, Marios, Table 10-11, p. 355.

[8] ibid.

[9] ibid.

[10] U.S. Census Bureau, 2002 Economic Census; Statistical Abstract of the United States, 2005.

Section 2

Chapter 5

[1] Simon, Julian, The Resourceful Earth 2 (Princeton, N.J.: Princeton University Press, 1996), pp. 41-52.

[2] Simon, Julian, ed., The State of Humanity (Oxford: Blackwell, 1995), Chapters 27 to 31.

[3] Energy Information Administration/Annual Energy Review, 2007 Tables 1.3 and 11.1.

[4] www.hubbertpeak.com/laherrere. Estimates of recoverable oil from oil shale are at 1.8 to 2 trillion barrels. Recoverable oil shale from the world is estimated to be about 2.6 trillion barrels. The Department of Energy estimates that the U.S. has over 6 trillion barrels of oil shale much of it insufficiently dense to be recoverable. Perhaps more could be recovered with improved technology in the future.

[5] ibid. Canada and Venezuela have an estimated 3.6 trillion barrels of oil in oil sands.(wikipedia.org)

[6] en.wikipedia.org/uranium There is an estimated 4.6 billion tons of uranium in the sea. Since the world uses about 40,000 tons per year, the sea contains enough uranium for 100,000 years at present levels of usage. If only 1 to 5 percent were recovered, there would be enough for 1000 to 5000 years at present levels of consumption.

[7] Department of Energy. Estimates of U.S. coal reserves are about 275 billion tons. But the U.S. may have as much as 4 trillion tons of coal in total (www.sourcewatch.com).

[8] en.wikipedia.org Official estimates of world coal reserves put it at 909 billion tons. However, Norway has 3 trillion tons under the North Sea much of which should be recoverable with development of the necessary technology. Probably worldwide there is at least 9 trillion tons of coal if undersea coal beds are included.

[9] en.wikipedia.org/uranium

[10] en.wikipedia.org/breeder reactor   Breeder reactors are being developed which will produce nearly as much or more nuclear fuel as they consume. They can reprocess waste uranium and use it providing additional thousands of years of nuclear fuel. In addition thorium is three times as plentiful as uranium and breeder reactors that use thorium primarily for fuel will also provide thousands of years of fuel for electricity and heat.

Chapter 6

[1] Michaels, Patrick, Climate of Extremes, pp. 2, 14.

[2] Michaels, Patrick, Meltdown (Washington, D.C.: Cato Institute, 2004), pp. 37-38.

[3] ibid. p. 10.

[4] ibid. pp.152-53, 166. From National Oceanic and Atmospheric Administration data.

[5] National Oceanic and Atmospheric Administration

[6] National Oceanic and Atmospheric Administration, Global Surface Temperature Anomalies, p. 4.

[7] Michaels, Climate of Extremes, pp. 43-55.

[8] ibid. p. 65.

[9] ibid. p. 62.

[10] Michaels, Meltdown, p.3.

[11] Huber, Peter W. and Mills, Mark P., The Bottomless Well (New York: Basic Books, 2005), p. 163

[12] Michaels, Patrick J. and Robert C. Balling Jr., Climate of Extremes (Washington, D.C.: Cato Institute, 2009), Chapter 7 discusses bias introduced by government officials.

Section 3

Chapter 7

[1] National Bureau of Economic Research, www.nber.org/cycles. html.

[2] Schumpeter, Joseph, Capitalism, Socialism, and Democracy (Scranton, Penn.: Harper Collins, 2008), pp 81-86.

[3] Keynes, John Maynard, General Theory.

[4] Folsom, Burton Jr., New Deal or Raw Deal? (New York: Simon and Schuster, 2008), p. 2.

Chapter 8

[1] Keynes, John Maynard, General Theory, pp. 15-16, 272-79. Keynes indicates how he differs from classical economists like A.C. Pigou.

[2] 2009 Economic Report of the President, Tables B-34, B-36, and B-40, and Statistical Abstracts of the United States.

[3] Keynes, pp 15-22.

Chapter 9

[1] National Bureau of Economic Research, www.nber.org/cycles. html.

[2] Keynes, pp. 372-382. Keynes recommended substantial government intervention in the economy in an ongoing basis to maintain spending and investment.

[3] Keynes, pp. 115, 120-21.

[4] Michael Boskin, Wall Street Journal, April 3, 2009.

Section 4

Chapter 10

[1] www.taxfoundation.org/files

[2] www.taxfoundation.org/files; Jorgenson, Dale W. and Landau, Ralph, eds. Tax Reform and the Cost of Capital, and King, Mervyn, and Don Fullerton, The Taxation of Income from Capital: A Comparative Study of the United States, United Kingdom, Sweden, and West Germany (Chicago: University of Chicago Press, 1984); KPMG Corporate and Individual Tax Rate Survey 2008; Central Statistics Office of Ireland; Corporate Tax Division, Inland Revenue Service of Singapore; and various other documents with information about corporate tax rates.

[3] United Nations Statistics 2006, Annual Average Rate of Growth of GDP by Major Area, Region, and Country, Table 4. United Nations System of National Accounts for earlier years.

[4] Keynes, p. 135.

Chapter 11

[1] www.taxfoundation.org/files

[2] Jorgenson, Dale W. and Landau, Ralph, eds. Tax Reform and the Cost of Capital, and King, Mervyn, and Don Fullerton, The Taxation of Income from Capital: A Comparative Study of the United States, United Kingdom, Sweden, and West Germany (Chicago: University of Chicago Press, 1984).

[3] U.S. Census Bureau, Census of Manufacturing 2002, Concentration Ratios in Manufacturing, p. 1.

[4] U.S. Census Bureau, Census of Manufacturing 1982, 1987, 1992, 1997, Concentration Ratios in Manufacturing.

[5] Statistical Abstract of the United States 2004-2005 (and earlier Abstracts), Table 741, p. 499.

[6] Returns for Domestic Non-Financial Business, Survey of Current Business 87 (May 2007); Note on Rates of Return for Nonfinancial Business, Survey of Current Business 79 (June 1999), Table 2.

[7] Statistical Abstract of the United States, various years; en.wikipedia. org/wiki/U.S._Automobile_Production_Figures; www.geocities.com/ fbessem/usa,html;
[8] www.usdoj.gov/atr/public/testimony/hhi.htm

Chapter 12

[1] IRS Statistics, Returns of Active Corporations, 1971-2006; Bicentennial Edition, Historical Statistics of the United States, Colonial Times to 1970, Part 2, Corporate Assets, Liabilities, and Income.

Chapter 13

[1] Pechman, Joseph, Federal Tax Policy, Fifth Ed. (Washington, D.C.: Brookings Institution, 1987), pp. 141-154.
[2] Bureau of Economic Analysis, NIPA Table 1.1.5, Fixed Asset Table 6.7.
[3] Bureau of Economic Analysis, NIPA Tables 1.14, 6.14A-D, 6.22A-D.
[4] Bureau of Economic Analysis, NIPA Tables 6.1A-D, 6.13A-D, 6.22A-D.
[5] Bureau of Economic Analysis, NIPA Tables 1.14, Fixed Asset Table 6.1.

Chapter 14

[1] U.S. Census Bureau, Census of Manufacturing 2002, Concentration Ratios in Manufacturing, p. 1.
[2] www.wikipedia.com

Chapter 15

[1] Michael Boskin, Wall Street Journal, April 3, 2009

Index